CHILDREN OF POVERTY

STUDIES ON THE EFFECTS
OF SINGLE PARENTHOOD,
THE FEMINIZATION OF POVERTY,
AND HOMELESSNESS

edited by

STUART BRUCHEY
UNIVERSITY OF MAINE

A GARLAND SERIES

THE IMPACT OF HOMELESSNESS ON CHILDREN

LINDA SULLIVAN

GARLAND PUBLISHING, Inc.
NEW YORK & LONDON / 1997

Library of Congress Cataloging-in-Publication Data

Sullivan, Linda, 1947–
    The impact of homelessness on children / Linda Sullivan.
        p.   cm. — (Children of poverty)
    Revision of the author's thesis (Ph. D.)—University of
Alabama at Birmingham, 1994.
    Includes bibliographical references and index.
    ISBN 0-8153-2762-5 (alk. paper)
    1. Homeless children—United States—Attitudes. 2. Home-
less children—Health and hygiene—United States. 3. Homeless
children—Medical care—United States. 4. Homelessness—United
States. I. Title. II. Series.
HV4505.S85 1997
362.7'086'942—dc21
                                                    96-39993

Printed on acid-free, 250-year-life paper
Manufactured in the United States of America

DEDICATION

This research is dedicated to all those children
who will never know the warmth of their own
home and who have lost their dreams. You
have challenged all of us to reach
into ourselves to help you find
your dreams again and
warm your nights.

Thank You !

Contents

TABLES

PREFACE

The trend toward an ever-increasingly younger population of homeless people is expected to continue. Families, usually mothers with children, now comprise the largest segment of the homeless population. The impact of the phenomenon of homelessness on a child has not been studied to date. While studies have been done to assess the health problems of homeless children, little else is known regarding the overall impact of this phenomenon on the child. The social, emotional, and spiritual impact, along with the impact on the physical well-being, needs to be better understood if nursing is to provide leadership in dealing with this ever growing population.

Utilizing a qualitative, phenomenological methodology, children between the ages of 9 and 12 years of age were interviewed. The research sought to answer the question: what are the meaning and significance of homelessness to a child? Rogers' Theory of Hemodynamics and Bandura's Social Learning Theory provided the theoretical framework for this research.

Homelessness has increased substantially over the last two decades. It is clear that as this country experiences more chronic poverty, there will continue to be an increase in the numbers of homeless individuals. Children are among those who are part of that rapidly increasing group of homeless individuals and it is often children who suffer the highest aggregate poverty rate of any age group in the United States.

The literature concerning homeless children strongly suggests that homelessness has a negative impact on many aspects of a child's life. The studies conducted thus far suggest that developmental delays, negative health outcomes, increased risk and severity of illnesses, and psychological problems are commonplace among homeless children.

While the literature gives health care providers information as to the nature and degree of various deficits in the health and overall well-being of homeless children, few studies exist that can assist the nurse in acquiring an understanding of the child's perception of homelessness. Much of the existing studies report on the parents perceptions only. If health care providers are to effectively address the needs of homeless children, it is important to understand the impact of the phenomenon of homelessness from the child's perspective. This study will provide information for health care providers working with homeless children which can facilitate a clearer understanding of the child's feelings about being homeless.

In the "land of plenty" is a sobering event when one has an opportunity to look into a child's eyes and see such intense sadness and longing for a place in this world. The children who are homeless, currently numbering approximately 300,000, have a myriad of unmet needs. These needs range from adequate, permanent housing, nutrition appropriate for their age, and basic health care opportunities, to a sense of permanence related to friends, educational opportunities and family.

Health care workers, teachers and social workers all need to remain cognizant of this unique "cultural" group. In a time where there is an increased awareness of cultural diversity between individuals and an increased sensitivity to the mode of delivery of care to these various cultural groups, it is imperative that the homeless be recognized as a unique culture.

Those who provide care or service to children should have a clear understanding of what it means to be homeless. While no one can ever fully comprehend the meaning and significance of homelessness, this study allowed the researcher to have a "birds eye view" of what it means to be a homeless child. Hopefully, this research will provide you with a clearer sense of homelessness from a child's point of view as you accompany them on their journey.

Linda Sullivan RN, CS, DSN
1996

ACKNOWLEDGMENTS

I would like to acknowledge the members of my committee for their guidance and patience during this research. These include Dr. Karen Newman, Dr. Penelope Wright, and Dr. Max Michael. A special thank you to Dr. Charlene McKaig who gave me continued encouragement throughout my graduate career. As both a member of my committee and my advisor Dr. McKaig always had the time to talk with me and assist me. Another special thanks to Dr. Elizabeth Stullenbarger who, as the chairperson of my committee, continually assisted me in completing this project. Her guidance, patience and friendship are greatly appreciated. Lastly, a very special thank you to my friend and mentor Dr. Jacob Skiwski. As a member of my committee, he always had time to listen to me, assist me in collecting my thoughts and ultimately help me in completing one more of my goals . . . to have my doctorate in nursing.

I would also like to thank both of the directors of the shelters Ms. Lida and Mr. George. Of course, a very special thanks to the children and their families for their cooperation, their trust in me and their honesty. Without their help this project would have never been completed.

To my colleagues at both Mississippi University for Women and the Children's Health Clinic thanks for your understanding during this research. I would also like to acknowledge and thank the Institutes of Higher Learning of Mississippi and Sigma Theta Tau, Zeta Rho Chapter for their financial support during my research and doctoral studies.

Finally, I would like to thank my family, Christine, Danielle and Michael Jr. and a special thanks to my husband Michael for all the encouragement, support and assistance in the completion of this project.

The Impact of Homelessness on Children

I

Introduction
to the Problem

Homelessness is not a new phenomenon but recent media attention has increased society's awareness of its magnitude. Until the 1980s the image most frequently associated with the homeless individual was a middle aged male who was alcohol and/or drug-dependent, living in the streets with bags in hand and begging for money.[1] This image, however, is no longer representative of the homeless population. Today, the fastest growing segment within this population is families with children.[2] Figures as high as three million homeless individuals are cited. These numbers are expected to grow exponentially within the next ten years, increasing the number of homeless to about six million.[3] The number of homeless families with children is currently estimated at 600,000.[4]

The National Governors' Association defined a homeless person as an undomiciled individual who is unable to secure permanent and stable housing without special assistance.[5] The reality is that it is no longer just those deemed mentally incompetent or involved in illicit practices who are homeless in today's population. Rather, it is a conglomerate of those new poor who, due to unemployment, violence (domestic or otherwise), or eviction, along with those who have problems with substance abuse and/or mental disorders, that presently comprise the largest part of the homeless population. Often, it is this group who have children living with them.

Although the literature abounds with information on the general area of homelessness, little attention has been paid to the homeless child. Homeless children are particularly at risk for physical,

3

social, emotional and developmental problems due to their dependence on adult care givers.[6]

Whereas some studies have sought to identify the most frequently encountered health problems among homeless children, none have looked at the meaning and significance that being homeless has on children's lives. Breakey & Fischer, who surveyed the health needs of homeless children at a New York City clinic, found that 25% were anemic, 50% had upper respiratory disorders, 29% had ear infections and 5% demonstrated serious growth failure.[7] The number of children surveyed, however, represented less that 12% of the estimated homeless children in that city. A particularly disturbing finding was that 4.7% of the children who were seen had active tuberculosis. The American Medical Association estimates that between 1.6 and 6.8 percent of all homeless individuals have active tuberculosis. This number represents a 300 times greater percentage of documented active tuberculosis cases than that found in the general population. While the study documented a multitude of health problems, it did not consider the psychological effects of the homeless experience on children.

Bassuk reported on various developmental and emotional problems of children living in family shelters in Massachusetts.[8] These children were found to have an increased incidence of serious psychological problems that included severe developmental lags, anxiety, depression and learning disabilities. Although specific health needs were not identified in this study, the investigator found that 21% of the children were reported to have had a major physical illness within the previous two years. This number is significantly higher than that found in the general pediatric population.[9]

Studies of both homeless children and adults have documented similar findings. The health profile (i.e. the complete health picture which includes not only physical problems but emotional and developmental problems as well) of homeless individuals is always poorer than that of the general population. While the same kinds of problems are encountered in the general pediatric population, the risk for the occurrence of these problems is significantly greater among the homeless.

Even when simple nutritional deficits in a child's diet are identified, shelters, a refuge for most of these children, are rarely able to provide the necessary nutritional supplements. Infants born to homeless women are also at risk. These infants have a 30% mortality rate and a two times greater likelihood of being a low birth weight infant.[10]

Homeless individuals seem to have a never-ending list of problems, but for homeless children, the plight is even more complicated. Studies have documented problems in parenting among homeless families, an increased incidence of abuse and neglect among homeless children,[11] and a lack of basic immunizations as well as abnormal physical and developmental growth.[12]

Access to health care is also a problem for homeless children. Often, even when clinics that service the needs of these children are present in the community, lack of transportation, money or parental understanding of the importance of health care, prevents utilization of the services. These problems, combined with existing inadequacies in available housing, affordable health care services, nutritional supplements, and the most basic of needs such as water, energy and space present difficult challenges for those who seek to provide services to this underserved population.

The saying "Children learn what they live" is supported by social learning theorists who note that children learn most of their behaviors, society's expectations and knowledge from the people with whom, and the environment in which they live.[13] For homeless children, their lived experience is filled with an increased risk for physical, emotional and developmental inadequacies. These risks in turn negatively affect the potential outcome for the child.

Research is needed that focuses upon improving expected outcomes for these clients. The first step is to understand the phenomenon of homelessness and the meaning and significance it has on children. Due to the lack of research related to the basic needs of homeless children, nursing could position itself to take a leadership role in understanding the impact of homelessness on children.

Research Question

This phenomenological, qualitative study sought to answer the question, "What are the significance and meaning of homelessness to the child?"

Assumptions

The assumptions that provided a basis for the theoretical background of this study are:
* The subjective experiences of homeless children provide legitimate, objective information.
* The homeless child's perceptions are multidimensional and a product of the immediate environment.
* The child's developmental and maturational level will affect perceptions and the ability to relate these perceptions to the researcher.

Definition of terms

The terms used in this study will be defined as follows:

HOMELESSNESS A state that exists when an individual is defined as being undomiciled and unable to secure permanent stable housing without special assistance.

Operational definition: Being without a permanent domicile for at least 2 weeks but not more than 6 months and currently residing in a shelter in Marietta, Georgia or Jackson, Mississippi.

MEANING AND SIGNIFICANCE The communicated perceptions of the lived experience of homelessness. These perceptions include expressed personal, cognitive, affective and physical responses of the child to his/her current situation of being without a permanent domicile.

Operational definition: Those communicated perceptions obtained through a semi-structured interview with a child, recorded on audio tape, transcribed and analyzed, and including observations made by the researcher.

CHILD A minor between the age of 7 and 12.

Operational definition: A minor between the ages of 7 and 12 who has no documented psychiatric problems and who lives with at least one parent in a homeless shelter.

Limitations

The following are acknowledged as potential limitations of the proposed study:

> * The interaction between the researcher and the child may influence the data gathering process as " . . .an interactive unity between the two exist."[14]
> * While an understanding of the patterns of homelessness in children will be achieved, the ability to generalize or predict is not expected.
> * The lack of experience of the researcher in performing research oriented interviews with children.

Conceptual Framework

Rogers' paradigm[15] and the Social Learning Theory will serve as the conceptual framework for this study. The emphasis of both of these theories on the effect and importance of the environment on an individual's potential for development will provide an appropriate framework through which the experience of homelessness for a child can be studied.

In Rogers' paradigm for nursing, the phenomena central to the purpose of nursing are people and the world in which they live. Rogers views human beings as unified whole and open systems which are in a constant state of exchange with the environment. People coexist in the universe with all things, living and non-living. As unitary human beings, individuals are associated with all other beings in their environment, whether that environment is arbitrarily defined as a home or a shelter.

The foundation of Rogers' model includes five basic assumptions:

> *Man is a unified whole possessing an individual integrity and exhibiting characteristics that are more than and different from, the sum of his parts (i.e. a synergistic being).
> * The individual and environment are continuously exchanging matter and energy with each other.
> * The life progression of an individual evolves along a space/time continuum.
> *Pattern and organization identify an individual and reflects his innovative wholeness.

> *Human beings are characterized by the capacity for
> abstraction, imagery, language, thought, sensation
> and emotion.[16]

The life process, in Rogers' view, is one of wholeness, continuity, and dynamic and creative change.

Rogers' theory is built upon the principles of hemodynamics which constitute three separate entities and in essence describe the life process.[17] *Integrality*, the first of these principles, describes the continuous, mutual and simultaneous interaction between human beings and the environment. *Helicy*, states that life proceeds in one direction of sequential and increasingly complex stages in the life continuum. The third, *resonancy*, deals with the continuous changes in the wave patterns between human beings and the environment.

The principles of hemodynamics predict the way that the life process proceeds and evolves. Rogers supports the belief that nursing practice should be one in which the practitioner strives to promote a balance between human beings and their environment. This is accomplished by strengthening the bond and the integrity of the human field while helping to correct those deficits in this reciprocal relationship.

Rogers further believes that maintenance and promotion of health are the two foremost responsibilities of nursing.[15] Nursing promotes and maintains health, evaluates therapeutic measures, and/or provides rehabilitative measures. The principles of hemodynamics rely heavily on observations pertaining to the mutual interactions of human beings and their environmental fields.

Similarly, Bandura's Social Learning Theory supports the importance of social variables as determinants of behavior and personality. Social variables which exert the most influence on an individual are the environment and models that are seen or heard. While social learning theorists do not stage development according to age, a child's development is viewed as an evolving process of cognitive and social growth. This process is defined by various stimulus that are unique for each child and the child's cognitive and social growth are a product of those variables exerted on an individual.

For the homeless child, living in an environment where even the most basic needs may not be met and where few role models exist from which to accrue information that might be incorporated in a gradual developmental process, the occurrence of a positive developmental process may face severe obstacles. New and complex appropriate behaviors are learned by observation. All behaviors, good and bad, can be assimilated into one's persona by simply observing them and their consequences. Behaviors and deficits in one's models cannot be altered or understood without recognizing one's social norms. Undesirable behaviors are often caused and subsequently reinforced by one's environment. Thus, effective treatment of a child living in an environment that has the potential to negatively influence his/her development, requires altering that environment or moving to a new "healthier" environment.

The effect of the environment, including all social variables that impact on the homeless child, is poorly understood.[18] A clearer understanding of the variables and the impact exerted on the homeless child can be facilitated by better understanding the lived experience of the homeless child.

A deficit in a child's interaction with the environment has the potential for having a negative impact on that child's potential development into adulthood. If a deficit in the child/environment relationship exists, the principles of integrality, helicy, and resonancy are all affected. When a deficit exists it must first be identified in order to develop a means to promote and maximize the child's interaction with that environment. This action, identification of the problem, can further serve to help develop a plan which has the ability to maximize the child's potential for optimal health.

For the homeless child, his or her interaction with the environment may have an impact on health, development, emotional and spiritual well-being. Rogers' paradigm can assist in understanding the effect that environment has on the potential for development into adulthood. When one incorporates both, Rogers' and Bandura's social learning theory, the full impact of environment on the ability to develop and realize one's fullest potential clearly seen.

The phenomenological approach allows the researcher to understand the interaction of the environment and the ability to develop fully from the subject's (homeless child) perspective. Rogers' paradigm provided the means to identify the effect of environment on the child and to evaluate the potential effect of that environment on the development of maximal health. Rogers' paradigm also allowed the researcher to accomplish the first step in correcting an imbalance through early identification of a problem in the child/environment interaction.

Notes

1. E. Bassuk and L. Rubin, "Homeless Children: A Neglected Population," *American Journal of Orthopsychiatry* 57(2)(1987): 279-286.

2. J. Wright and E. Weber, *Homelessness and Health* (New York, N.Y.:McGraw Hill, 1988).

3. D. R. Hodnicki, "Homelessness: Health Care Implications," *Journal of Community Health Care* 7(2)(1990):59-67.

4. D. Kinzel, "Self identified Health Concerns of Two Homeless Groups," *Western Journal of Nursing Research* 13(2)(1991):181-184.

5. United States Congress, House of Delegates, Select Committee on Hunger, *Hunger among the Homeless: A Survey of 140 Shelters, Food Stamp Participation and Recommendations* (Washington, D.C.:United States Government, 1987), 7-40.

6. E. Bassuk and L. Rosenberg, "Psychosocial Characteristics of Homeless Children and Children with Homes," *Pediatrics* 85(3)(1990):257-261.

7. W. Breakey and P. Fischer, "Down and Out in a Land of Plenty," *Johns Hopkins Magazine* 37(1985):16-24.

8. E. Bassuk, "The Homeless Population," *Scientific American* 251(1)(1984):40-45.

9. R. Parker, L. Rescoria, J. Finklestein, and N. Barnes, "A Survey of Health of Homeless Children in Philadelphia Shelters," *American Journal of Diseases in Children* 14(1991):20-526.

10. S. Damrosche, P. Sullivan, A. Scholler, and J. Gaines, "On Behalf of Homeless Families," *Journal of Maternal Child Nursing* 13(5)(1988):256-263.

11. L. J. Pearson, "Providing Health Care to the Homeless-Another Important Role for NP's," *Nurse Practitioner* 13(4)(1988): 38-48.

12. A. Casey, "An Oasis in the Streets," *California Nurses Review* 11(1)(1989):p.46.

13. A. Bandura, *Social Learning Theory* (Englewood Cliffs, N.J.:Prentice Hall, 1977).

14. J. Haase and S. Myers, "Reconciling Paradigm Assumptions of Qualitative Research, "*Western Journal of Nursing Research* 10(2)(1988):128-137.

15. M. Rogers, *Visions of Science Based Nursing* (New York: National League for Nursing, 1990).

16. M. Rogers, *An Introduction to the Theoretical Basis of Nursing* (Philadelphia:F. A. Davis, 1970).

17. A. Marriner, *Nursing Theorists and Their Work* (St. Louis: C. V. Mosby, 1986).

18. L. Rescoria, R. Parker, and P. Stolley, "Ability, Achievement and Adjustment in Homeless Children," *American Journal of Orthopsychiatry* 6(2)(1991):210-220.

II

Review of Literature

This review focuses upon research studies related to homeless children conducted within the last fifteen years. The studies were identified by an extensive hand and computer search including Grateful Med, Medline and Silver Platter, and CINAHL. During this search only nine research articles were identified. Most of the research conducted to date has concentrated on describing the personal and physical characteristics, as well as other demographic features, of the homeless population. No studies were identified that sought to provide an understanding of the phenomenon of homelessness from the child's perspective, nor did any of the studies examine the emotional or psychological impact that this phenomenon had on the child. The research articles that were identified focused on health care needs and developmental assessment issues which were identified by homeless children or the parents of these children. The findings of the nine research articles will be discussed.

Research/Homeless Children

Murata, Mace, Strehlow & Shuler[1] conducted a social epidemiological study which compared the health problems of severely impoverished homeless children to the health problems of children for whom visits to a pediatric clinic were reimbursed (NAMSC). The study also described the changes needed for the delivery of effective nursing care among those identified as severely impoverished. The inductive method was utilized and sought to generate hypotheses about the causes that lead to a state of health or disease.

The study was conducted at two separate sites. One site was in Los Angeles at a health care center for homeless children. The center, operated by nurse practitioners, averaged 825 visits per month. The second site was a private pediatric clinic in the same geographic area which had a total of 2035 visits.

The sample included 303 visits by homeless children during a seven month period to a pediatric clinic and a comparable sampling from the NAMSC group. The children in both groups were all less than 18 years of age. Diagnoses were those described by the ICD-9-CM diagnostic and demographic categories for both the homeless group and the NAMSC group. The diagnoses were divided into 5 groups: acute diseases, communicable diseases, chronic diseases, prevention and injury care.

Data analysis was accomplished by proportion analysis, the Z test, an epidemiological statistical test and other inferential statistics. Demographically, the groups were equal for gender; examination of ethnicity found that a greater percentage of minorities (24.0%) existed in the homeless group when compared to the NAMCS group (10.2%). Over one-half (54.6%) of the NAMCS group were less than 5 years old while the mean age of the homeless group was 8.46. Residence varied in the homeless group and included the street (17%), shelters (8%), skid row hotels (27%) and substandard housing (35%). All participants in the NAMCS group lived in a home with their own family or their extended family.

Five percent of the homeless group and 100% of those in the NAMCS group had an identified means of paying for health care visits which included medicaid, medicare, self- pay or insurance. Statistical analysis revealed that the homeless sample had a lesser proportion of visits attributed to communicable disease, disease prevention and injury; however, more visits for acute diseases were made by the NAMCS group. The greater proportion of the visits for the NAMCS group were related to age (*i.e.* younger children) and access to health care, as most of the visits were related to well-baby care. There was an increase in serous otitis in homeless children and this was suggested to be a result of untreated upper respiratory infections and pharyngitis.[1]

In the category of communicable disease, Murata et al. hypothesized that the decreased number of visits by homeless children was due to a belief held by their families that the problems were self-limiting and that the urgent needs of food, shelter, and clothing superseded health promotion needs. The greatest differences between the groups were found to be related to the significantly higher number of infections, particularly pediculosis and scabies, found in the homeless group, which was believed to be related to the living conditions.

With regard to preventive care, the most significant difference was found when screening for tuberculosis (TB), with nearly a 25 times greater incidence of TB found in the homeless group. Injuries were also greater in the homeless sample, with open wound and lacerations being most prominent followed in frequency by sprains and strains. The researchers believed these increases were attributable to the greater risks in the environment. No specific frequencies or percentages were given to identify how often these problems occurred.

With regard to the second purpose of the study the results showed that differences did exist between the two groups and these were a result of the environmental conditions and social policies currently in existence. Furthermore, the results suggested that health care providers would have to adjust the plan of care to meet the environmental constraints of the client and modify these approaches as needed.

This study concluded that it had definitely demonstrated that nursing clinics, which are both cost effective and efficient, can meet the needs of the homeless population. Nurses, therefore, need to act as client advocates for these children and should provide comprehensive, coordinated health care as this is a right of every child.

Although the results speak directly to nursing's role in the care of special populations, little statistical evidence was presented that supported the second purpose. One should note that nearly all the health problems and deficits were stated to be related to environment or other access problems. Murata et al. recommended that more work related to meeting the needs of impoverished children be done by nurses at the local, state and national level.

Adkins and Fields sought to identify the health care values of homeless women and their children.[2] Health care values were those reasons that one does or does not seek health care. A descriptive study utilizing the Health Belief Model as the theoretical framework was conducted in order to determine the reasons for a seeming lack of motivation for health care maintenance among the homeless population. The sample included 10 mothers with their children who volunteered to take part in the study. The median age of the sample was 26.5. Eighty percent (80) were black and 20 percent (2) were white, which was stated to be representative of the area. The work history revealed that seven were currently working and three were attending school. The average length of stay in the shelter was 9.6 months. The average number of children in each family was 1.8 and the children ranged in age from six months to 18 years. Utilizing an interview guide that consisted of seven questions, each woman was encouraged to express her views related to health care issues. The interviews, which were tape recorded and subsequently analyzed, lasted between 30 and 45 minutes.

The results of the study were categorized according to the Health Belief Model.[2] The results of the study indicated that the subject's prior experiences with the health care system had been positive during their childhood years. The main difference between the groups was that, at this point in their lives, perceived needs had to be classified as an emergency before health care was sought. This was often due to the lack of money or the large number of other more pressing needs. The perceived benefits were only those that could be seen to meet the actual needs of survival. Health maintenance and prevention of illness were not seen as benefits due to the overwhelming nature of their current situation.

The results of the study showed that the perceived barrier identified by the majority of the subjects was access to health care. Access was qualified by the following modifiers: long waits, accompanied by being treated by unfamiliar health care providers; having to miss work in order to seek the care; and the lack of available HMO type facilities which made access difficult for this population.

Adkins and Fields recommended that a plan be adopted that would assist the homeless mother in "getting through" the difficulties which accompanied securing health care for themselves and their children. The authors further recommended that programs be instituted which emphasized the importance of preventive health activities. They also pointed out the need for establishing health care centers on site at homeless shelters to help control the spread of communicable disease and provide early intervention for other health related problems. Finally, Adkins & Fields noted the need to increase utilization of the

McKinley Homeless Assistance Act, which to date is meeting only 15% of the health care needs of the homeless population.

J. Bass, P. Brennan, K. Mehta, and S. Kodzis conducted a descriptive study which sought to better quantify the health problems of children in an suburban Massachusetts homeless shelter.[3] The purpose of the study was to validate the efficacy of an affiliation between a hospital-based clinic and a homeless shelter for families.

A shelter in Framington, Massachusetts, which lies 20 miles outside of Boston, was the setting for this study. Data were collected from December 1986 to December 1987. The sample included 78 children from 43 families. Ages of the subjects ranged from 0 to 18 years. Newborns to one year old children represented 18% of the sample, 2 to 5 year olds, 40%, 6 to 12 year olds, 33% and 13 to 18 year olds, 9%. Ninety-nine percent of these children received all their health care at the clinic associated with the shelter.

The methodology involved having each child participate with their parent(s) in an intake screening and questioning session which was conducted by a member of the hospital clinic staff. Then a comprehensive pediatric history was taken, followed by a physical exam. Additionally, a Mantoux, stool culture, ova and parasite study, free erythrocyte protoporphyrin (if < 6 years of age) and hemoglobin were done for each new resident.

Stool cultures were positive for Giardia lamblia (13% children and 9% adults) Salmonella B (2 children), Aeromonas hydrophila (2 children) and Shigella sonnei (1 adult). All but one of these were asymptomatic.[3] Overall, 65% of children and 44% of adults had one or more acute or chronic health problems. The types of problems found included communicable diseases (chicken pox and lice), routine infant problems (otitis and dermatitis), incomplete immunizations, developmental problems, and abuse.

Fifty-eight percent of the sample were not only homeless but "medically homeless" (*i.e.* the children had no means of meeting the most basic health needs), despite the fact that nearly all subjects were eligible for medicaid.

Bass et al. concluded that, given the large number of identified and potential health problems, the affiliation between the hospital clinic and the shelter filled a significant need for this population thus validating the efficacy of health care facilities in shelters. This affiliation allowed those in the shelter to appropriately and adequately meet their health care needs. The affiliation between the clinic and shelter could therefore serve as an entry point for the family into a health care system.

Bassuk and Rosenberg conducted a case control study for the purpose of describing and comparing the psychosocial characteristics of homeless children and children with homes.[4] The sample included 86 children from 49 homeless families and 134 children from 81 housed families. The mean age of the mothers was 28 and children 2.4 years. One-third of the total sample was white with the majority of the remaining population black. These demographics reflected a significant under representation of Hispanics which was due to the researcher's inability to obtain access to one shelter that primarily housed Hispanic families. Data collection took place from April 1986 to July 1986.

Bassuk and Rosenberg had the parents complete behavioral checklists and standardized instruments which were used to assess the children. The Simmons Behavior Checklist, Denver Developmental Screening Test (DDST), Children's Depression Inventory, Children's Manifest Anxiety Scale and the Child Behavioral Checklist were the instruments utilized in this study. No reliability or validity for these instruments were given.

Data were analyzed using Chi-square and *t*-tests in order to assess the statistical significance of differences between children who were homeless and those with homes. Significance was set at the 0.05 level.

It was found that marital status, age and ethnicity were similar in both groups. Homeless families reported that they moved more often, citing an average of 4 moves in the previous year. More of those mothers with homes than those without (34 versus 11) reported that the fathers of the children were somewhat financially responsible for the children. Twenty-seven percent of the homeless group were being investigated for abuse. Severe emotional problems were found in 35% homeless and 24% housed children. Fifteen percent of homeless versus 19% of housed were reported to have chronic illnesses.

Results on the DDST showed that 54% of homeless and 16% of housed children exhibited developmental delays. These percentages were similar across ethnic, gender and race. Results from the Behavioral Checklist consistently showed that homeless children did worse in school (36%), more frequently repeated a grade (40%) or were presently failing a grade (36%) than those children who were classified as housed.

On the Manifest Anxiety Scale, 31% of homeless children scored 60 or greater indicating the need for psychiatric referral. One-third of the homeless children compared to one-tenth of the housed children showed the need for further follow up in this area. The Children Depression Inventory index showed similar results for both groups which further substantiated the need for follow-up.

Although both groups (homeless and housed) were below the poverty index, some differences were attributed to frequent moves, the lack of positive role models and other life experiences associated with homelessness. Overall, fewer differences were found than expected which may be attributed to their similar economic levels. The only areas that revealed statistically significant differences were in the scores on the DDST and school performances of the children.

The researchers recommended the development of long range policies which could appropriately respond to the diverse needs of both the poor and the homeless child. The results strongly suggested that attention be given to the emotional, medical, educational and social needs of these children so as to intervene in problems that could "cripple their ability to function."

In an earlier study, Bassuk and Rubin assessed 156 homeless children in order to validate the description of homeless shelters given by providers, advocates and researchers.[5] These descriptions stated that the living conditions in the shelter were very poor and were in need of change if shelters were to be effective. The researchers systematically collected clinical information about each child relating to his/her developmental, emotional, behavioral and learning problems.

The sample included 83 families and 156 children. The children were nearly all the same gender (boys) and aged between 6 weeks and 18 years although the majority (65%) were less than 5 years old. The families were primarily single parented (90%) by mothers whose average age was 27. Each family had an average of 2.4 children.

Following receipt of informed consent each mother was given a 55 item questionnaire. The questionnaire sampled demographic, medical and psychiatric information and provided a description of family relationships and a profile of school and school- related activities of the children. Researchers administered the DDST, Simmons

Behavioral Checklist, Children's Manifest Anxiety Scale and
Achenbach Behavioral Problem Checklist. All data were statistically
analyzed as suggested by the protocols of the individual instruments.

Bassuk and Rubin found that on the DDST 47% of the children
exhibited one area of developmental delay, 33% two to three areas and
14% had four or more areas.[5] Scores on the Children's Depression
Inventory were 10.4, indicating a need for psychiatric referral and
evaluation. An average score of 5.6 for the Simmons Behavior
Checklist was significantly higher than expected for a sample of
"normal" children. Problems identified included sleep disorders and
withdrawn and/or aggressive behaviors. The results were supported by
scores achieved on the Children's Manifest Anxiety Scale and the
Achenbach Behavioral Checklist, which indicated that the children were
more depressed and anxious, often displaying aggressive personalities.

The majority (60%) of mothers received aid for dependent
children (AFDC) and had little emotional support from family members
or significant others (24%). Approximately 20% of the mothers were
under investigation for child abuse and neglect, and approximately 34%
were themselves abused. Nine percept of the children were in therapy
or counseling and 25% viewed their mothers as emotionally or mentally
ill.

This study showed that a large number of the children
experienced developmental delays, anxiety and depression as well as
multiple learning disabilities. Bassuk and Rubin related these problems
directly to the stressful environment of the shelters, recommending that
appropriate social policies be developed which address the multiple
stressors that impact on the homeless population.[5] The researchers felt
that without immediate intervention the future of homeless children
would be seriously jeopardized.

Bassuk and Rosenberg [6] expanded on the earlier work of Bassuk
and Rubin by studying children classified as impoverished and homeless
children. In this study the developmental achievements of children of
homeless families headed by women were compared with those of
children in families who were poor, housed and headed by single
mothers. A non-random sample was used in this case control study.
The authors statistically analyzed data originally collected by Bassuk
and Rubin so that a comparison of the two groups could be
accomplished. As described previously, the homeless sample consisted
of 86 children residing with only their mothers in a homeless shelter in

the Boston area. The comparison group consisted of 134 poor children living in homes in the Boston area headed by women.

Informed consent, standardized behavioral checklists and demographic information about these children were completed by the mothers only. Data were collected with instruments which measure behavioral and psychological parameters. Preschool children were evaluated using the Denver Developmental Screening Test (DDST) and the Simmons Behavioral Checklist. School-aged children were tested using the Children's Depression Inventory, Children's Manifest Anxiety Scale, and the Child Behavioral Checklist. Data were analyzed using the chi square test to determine significant differences in test scores between the two groups.

A higher proportion of preschool homeless children displayed developmental lags in each of the four areas measured by the DDST. The scores for the two groups were similar in the Simmons Behavioral Checklist and the Depression Inventory. While scores for the Child Behavioral Checklist and Children's Manifest Anxiety Scale were slightly higher for homeless children, there were no statistically significant differences between the two groups.

Bassuk and Rosenberg concluded that differences in the DDST scores were directly related to homelessness and the environment to which the homeless children were exposed.[6] The researchers recommended that measures be provided for both the homeless and the child living in poverty that would assist these children in meeting basic developmental needs.

Rescoria, Parker, and Stolley assessed intellectual ability, academic achievement, and emotional/behavioral adjustment of a group of homeless children.[7] A second group, which also lived in the inner city, included poor but housed children for comparison purposes. The researchers were concerned with two specific problems: the lack of research which dealt with the status of homeless and impoverished children as well as the conflicting results of those few that had been completed. Rescoria et al. reported that homelessness and poverty had a significant negative impact on the quality of life for both the homeless and poor children.

The sample was chosen at random from a roster of a homeless shelter and the waiting room of a pediatric clinic in Philadelphia's inner city area. The sample consisted of 83 shelter children and 45 clinic children, 95 % of whom were black and whose ages ranged from 3 to

12 years. Ten standardized instruments were administered which assessed verbal and non-verbal intelligence, academic achievement, visual-motor development, and behavioral/emotional functioning. The preschool children were assessed using the Draw a Person Test, Three Wishes, and the Achenbach Child Behavioral Checklist. School aged children were evaluated by the WISC-R Vocabulary, Block Design, WHAT-R Reading Subtest, Stafford-Binet Vocabulary Test, Peabody Picture Vocabulary Test, Beery Developmental Test, and Cubes Test. Descriptive statistics were used to analyze the data from cognitive testing for both groups. Behavioral-emotional responses were measured using an externalizing score with each child receiving a total problem score.

Rescoria et al. found that preschool homeless children were significantly more delayed in receptive vocabulary ($t(55)=-2.23$, p. < .05) and visual-motor development ($t(46)=-2.04$, p. <.05) than poor inner city children. The homeless children also had significantly higher rates of behavioral/emotional symptoms ($t(56)= 3.96$, p >.001) than children of similar age and background living in homes. There were no significant differences among the preschool groups on the receptive vocabulary test and the visual-motor ability test. Scores of school-aged children living in shelters were not different than those of housed children for all categories tested.

Rescoria et al. attributed differences for the preschool group to the fact that 85% of the preschool homeless subjects did not attend any type of day care whereas 65% of the inner city children did. The researchers suggested that children who spent their formative years in shelters appeared to be particularly vulnerable to the negative effects of homelessness. Recommendations from this study included day care for all poor and homeless children so as to increase the potential for their development.

Terrell examined differences in developmental levels between poor and homeless children at two separate sites in rural Mississippi.[8] The first was a homeless shelter in which the clients lived in a communal environment with 10 other families. The second setting was a waiting room in the local health department. Twenty children between the ages of 2 months and 5 years, were included in the sample. The children were evaluated only with the Denver Developmental Screening Test. Parse's Theory provided the theoretical framework for this study. Parents were also interviewed in order to obtain their perception of the child's developmental progress. Although the homeless children scored consistently lower (failed more areas) than the poor children, there were no significant statistical differences noted. However, despite the lack of significant differences, all of the parents in the homeless group felt that their children were slower than other children. When asked why they felt this to be true, the parents identified the poor environment, lack of toys and day-care, and poor health of the children as the most significant contributors to developmental delays.

It is important to note here that the parents' perceptions centered around environmental deficits and their effects on the children. Parse's theory supports the role of environment in the actualization of maximal or optimal goals of an individual. In case and fact the homeless children did score lower than the poor children and while not statistically significant, Terrell proposed that the environment was the one factor that was different between the two groups and therefore may have contributed to the poorer developmental skills of the homeless children.

Bass et al. examined the experiences related to the delivery of care to pediatric clients in a homeless shelter. Their purpose was to assist health care providers in formulating a basic framework which would serve as a guide when providing needed medical services for homeless children. The researchers chose to concentrate on the pediatric client as it was their belief that the existing literature had concentrated almost exclusively on the experiences of adult clients in a shelter. The setting was in a Massachusetts shelter that communally housed families who were classified as homeless. The shelter directors had identified the rampant spread of communicable diseases as one of the most pressing problems within the shelter. The most common health care problems identified were ear infections, upper respiratory problems, diarrhea, anemia, hepatitis, chicken pox, head and body lice, a variety of skin problems and conjunctivitis.

As part of the study, the researchers,[3] along with a multidisciplinary team consisting of nurses, physicians, social workers and religious workers, entered the shelter in an effort to not only identify problems but to improve the health care status of the residents. A comprehensive medical intake program was initiated which included evaluation of developmental needs of the children. The primary goals of this program were to treat the families who were identified as having easily transmissible diseases before entering the shelter so as to decrease the spread of communicable diseases, provide ongoing care for residents, update routine primary care needs of families with children and to provide a medical home base for individuals that did not have a regular primary care provider.

Descriptive data were collected for one year based on a sample of 78 children from 43 families. Sixty-five percent of the children had one or more acute or chronic problems including learning disorders, developmental delays and language problems. Seventy eight percent of the population remained within the shelter health care system after leaving the shelter. Bass et al. concluded that incorporating a medical intake program upon entrance to a shelter, with subsequent treatment of identified problems, significantly reduced the spread and outbreaks of disease in a shelter. The researchers reported no occurrences of secondary infection at the shelter during the first year of this intervention. Additionally, by admitting this population to a health care system, there was a long-term positive effect on their overall health.

Recommendations included evaluation of the medical needs of all homeless persons prior to admission to a shelter by a multidisciplinary team in an effort to improve health for those in and entering the shelter. The authors also felt that special emphasis needed to be placed on the children's physical and emotional health so as to decrease the emotional and developmental problems often found in this group.

Notes

1. J. Murata, J. Mace, A. Stretlow, and P. Schuler, *Journal of Pediatric Nursing* 7(3)(1992):196-203.

2. C. Adkins and J. Fields, "Health Care Values of Homeless Women and Their Children," *Family and Community Health* (1992).

3. J. Bass, P. Brennan, K. Mehta, and S. Kodzis, "Pediatric Problems in a Suburban Shelter for Homeless Families," *Pediatrics* 85(1)(1990):33-39.

4. E. Bassuk and L. Rosenberg, "Psychosocial Characteristics of Homeless Children and Children with Homes," *Pediatrics* 85(3)(1990): 257-261.

5. E. Bassuk and L. Rubin, "Homeless Children: A Neglected Population," *American Journal of Orthopsychiatry* 57(2)(1987): 279-286.

6. E. Bassuk and L. Rosenberg, "Why Does Family Homelessness Occur? A Case-Control Study," *American Journal of Public Health* 78(7)(1988):783-388.

7. L. Rescoria, R. Parker, and P. Stolley, "Ability, Achievement and Adjustment in Homeless Children," *American Journal of Orthopsychiatry* 6(2)(1991):210-220.

8. C. Terrell, *Developmental Levels of Children who are Classified as Homeless and Children who are not Classified as Homeless* (1993)(Unpublished master's thesis, Mississippi University for Women, Columbus, MS).

III

Methodology

This study addressed the question, "What are the meaning and significance of homelessness to a child?" This chapter provides an overview of the qualitative methodology and a description of the instruments utilized. The setting, population and sample are described, as well as a description of the method of data collection and analysis.

Design

The phenomenological method was utilized for this study because the primary objective of the research was to facilitate an understanding of the phenomenon from the perspective of those being studied. When studying a complex phenomenon, an exploration of the subjective experiences of a group of individuals provides the researcher with valid information about the phenomenon of interest.[1] This methodology addresses the nature of a particular phenomenon as humanly recognized.[2]

The phenomenological method focuses attention on the perceptions and experiences of the participants or subjects. The detailed descriptions which result provide the basis for an inductive analysis.[3] Utilizing a phenomenological methodology allowed the researcher an effective means to better understand the homeless child's experience. Furthermore, it assisted the researcher in achieving a better understanding of the meaning and significance of the phenomenon of homelessness to a child.

Instrumentation

A review of the literature related to interviewing techniques with children as well as the environmental and personal factors that impact on a child's life was conducted prior to construction of the tool. The purpose of the review was to better understand both the mechanics of the interview process and to identify those factors that have an impact on a child's life.

Often, when trying to assess a child's feelings and perceptions, researchers have concentrated on the caregivers (*i.e.* parents, teachers, etc.), who have then become the primary respondent regarding the thoughts and feelings of the child.[4] Faux stated that qualitative methodologies, specifically those involving interviewing children and adolescents, can be successfully applied.[5] Furthermore, when the child is the primary respondent, the credibility of the research is significantly enhanced. Becker[6] and Lofland & Lofland stated that, particularly in qualitative studies where one is seeking to gain an understanding of an individual's perceptions and feelings, the data is far more valid when obtained from the subjects themselves.

In this study an interview was conducted with each child in order to achieve a better understanding of the lived experience of homelessness from their perspective. The use of a semistructured tool, the interview guide, facilitated this method of data gathering and has been found to facilitate an individual's ability to describe the subjective perspective of his or her life.[7] Interviewing is an appropriate method as long as the interview is centered on the individual's experiences.[8]

While few studies have tested the assertion that, within certain age limitations, information gathered from a child is valid and reliable, many authors have indicated this to be true.[9] School age children (7 to 12 years old) are competent reporters of their own life experiences but may present unique challenges to the interviewer.[10] The literature supports the belief that questions should be of such a nature that paraphrasing, in order to adapt to a particular child's linguistic ability, will not change the meaning of the question. The interviewer should clarify responses given by a child to validate those responses. While it is true that a child who is 7 and one who is 12 may have different linguistic abilities, children in these age groups have the capacity to understand and respond to questions related to their life experiences.

Issues related to the actual construction of the interview guide were then explored. First, the decision to use a semi-structured guide was made. A semi-structured guide is one that has flexibility and can be adapted to the variability in linguistic abilities and comprehension of each child without significantly changing the meaning of each of the questions.[12] This practice was supported in the extensive work of Munson & Munson, who demonstrated that this form of interview, free or semi-structured, resulted in significantly more reliable results.[13]

The questions themselves were designed to identify those variables which impact a child's development. In order to identify these variables, a conceptual map was constructed which helped to develop a common frame of reference for the children. A conceptual map assists the researcher in developing a common frame of reference through which one uncovers information relevant to the problem being researched. A conceptual map is designed by incorporating information learned from literature, along with pertinent observations of the researcher relevant to the problem being studied. The conceptual map identified the antecedent, mediating and outcome variables. Antecedent variables included emotional response to homelessness, the dramatic increase in the numbers of homeless children, the severity of the problem and the inadequate resources currently available to deal with the problem. Mediating variables, included orientation, education, sociological response, psychosocial response, spirituality, biological and environment. Lastly, outcome variables were identified. These included increasing the knowledge base for health care providers of homeless children, improving health outcomes for the children, and providing assistance in the development of anticipatory strategies when dealing with the children. In the construction of the interview guide only the mediating variables were addressed and incorporated into the questions since these factors should most impact on the lived experience of homelessness for a child.

The questions were then devised so that those factors identified through the conceptual map could be addressed. Additionally, factors relevant to the development of a child during the school age years were also incorporated. Those developmental factors included issues related to family, friends, physical, spiritual and school performance.

The researcher served as the primary instrument in this study. Additionally, a researcher-designed interview guide was used (Appendix A). The interview guide was composed of 14 questions which addressed personal, social, religious, emotional, familial and physical factors that were thought to influence the development of a child. The interview guide was used to facilitate a conversation with each child who participated in the study. Content validity of this guide was established by a panel of experts consisting of two homeless shelter coordinators, a pediatrician and three family nurse practitioners whose practice was primarily with young children.[15]

The tool was pilot-tested in a homeless shelter with five children serving as the subjects. Following the pilot testing, two questions were added to the interview guide. These were, "What does the word homeless mean to you?" and "Where is your home?" Initially, children between the ages of seven and 12 were to be included in the study. Two seven year olds participated in the pilot-test. The interviews with two of the seven year old children were then excluded and subsequently no other six year old children were interviewed. There was a reluctance from the seven year old children to speak and respond to the majority of questions that were asked thus rendering these interviews unusable in the research study. The researcher observed that the material gathered in these two interviews was both incomplete and difficult to analyze and this was thought to be a function of their age. A tape recorder was used to record all interviews.

Setting

There were two settings for this study. The first was a shelter for homeless families located in south central Mississippi. The shelter is funded by 12 separate churches and no federal funds are encumbered for the operation of the shelter. The shelter is a converted two story home, located in Jackson, Mississippi, in a city of approximately 300,000 people. The house has seven oversized bedrooms, a communal kitchen, playroom, social room and four bathrooms. The shelter can house up to 25 people. At the time of data collection one of the bedrooms was unoccupied and thus served as a quiet place in which to conduct the interviews with the children. Although adequate seating was available in this room, each child chose to sit on the floor and thus the researcher followed suit.

The second setting for conduction of the research was a family shelter located in northwest Georgia, in a city of approximately 825,000 people. The shelter is supported by the Methodist Ministries and receives no federal funding. The physical setting consisted of one main building in which the residents sleep, a clinic operated on Tuesday and Thursday evenings in a trailer located behind the main house, a smaller building which serves as a playroom or respite space for children and women during the day when the shelter is closed (7 AM to 4:30 PM), a dining hall and a clothing building. The main house included double and triple decker bunk beds arranged within three feet of each other. Pallets or mattresses on the floor along with three cribs are available for children. In most cases the children slept with their mothers. There is a partition to separate the men from the women and children and a communal bathroom with two showers and three bathroom stalls. The shelter can house up to 65 adults and 15 children although the director stated that often there were more than 15 children. The researcher was welcomed at both shelters. Both directors expressed hope that effective interventions might be brought about for these children when attention was placed on their experience.

Population and Sample

The population included all homeless children between the ages of seven and twelve, currently residing in one of two family shelters in Mississippi or Georgia whose parents consented and who themselves gave their assent to participate in the study. The sample included nine children who met the criteria for inclusion in the study. Additional criteria for inclusion in the study were that the children had no documented psychiatric illness and were in residence at the shelter for at least two weeks but not more than six months. This information was gained from each of the shelter directors and verified by the parent of each child.

Adequacy of the sample was achieved when redundancy or saturation of the description of the homeless experience was achieved. Redundancy is realized when repetition of the same descriptions of a phenomenon are related and no new information is given by the subjects.

The subject's human rights were protected and anonymity was provided to all participants. All children were asked to sign or verbally assent to participate in the study (Appendix B) following an explanation of the study and the procedure to be employed in the research. Each parent was asked to sign a consent form following an explanation of the study (Appendix C). It was explained that no risks were involved for the subjects and that there were no immediate benefits to the children either. Parents were told that the information gained through this research might facilitate delivery of improved health care for homeless children, provide an anticipatory needs guide and identify needed information to health care providers working with homeless children.

Data Collection Procedure

Permission to conduct the study was obtained from the Institutional Review Board (IRB) at the University of Alabama in Birmingham. A full review was conducted by the board and permission was granted (Appendix D). Following IRB approval, the two shelters were contacted. The administrators of each shelter were contacted by phone and then in person and a letter was obtained from both (Appendices E and F) which granted the researcher permission to conduct interviews with homeless children residing in the shelters.

Dates to conduct the interviews were arranged and data collection took place between October 1992 and July 1993. The procedure followed for each interview was to arrive either after school hours or on the weekend at one of the shelters. A brief discussion with the administrators was held to identify children who met the criteria for inclusion. Following this activity the researcher met with each child and his or her parent. The purpose of the study was explained to both the parent and the child. When talking with the children every effort was made to use developmentally appropriate language. Assent from each child and consent from each parent was then obtained.

The child then accompanied the researcher to a separate room where the interview was conducted. Each child was given a few moments to get comfortable with the room, researcher and equipment (tape recorder). The child was then asked if he or she was ready to proceed and the interview began. Several children were reluctant at first to speak and the tape recorder was shut off. The process was then explained again to the child. In no instance was it necessary to turn the tape recorder off for more than five minutes. All children were eventually able to proceed but occasionally had to be reminded that they needed to verbalize their responses rather than act them out (*i.e.* shrugging, nodding, smiling). All audio-taped recordings were conducted in a private space within the shelter and no one but the researcher and the transcription typist had access to the tape recordings. Following transcription, all tapes were destroyed.

The interviews consisted of the researcher following the interview guide to facilitate obtaining descriptions of the impact of the homeless experience for the child. The interviews lasted from 12 to 35 minutes. Care was taken to keep the interviews as brief as possible while still allowing the subject's adequate time to express themselves as suggested by Faux et al. Subtle clues of anxiety or fatigue were acknowledged by the researcher as an indication that the interview needed to be brought to a conclusion.

Field notes were taken by the researcher during each interview. These notes supplemented the audiotaped responses and recorded physical and affective responses of the children. Transcriptions of the tape recordings were done, single-spaced on one half of each page vertically. Each line was numbered and field notes added in the right margins at appropriate places. Analysis of the data was then conducted following van Kaam's methodology.[15]

Analysis of the Data

Analysis of the data was accomplished through a rigorous, systematic approach employing the methodology of van Kaam.[15] This method includes six major activities that were the guiding principles for data analysis. These activities are:

* eliciting descriptive expressions
* identifying common elements
* eliminating those expressions not related to the phenomenon
* formulating a hypothetical definition of the phenomenon
* applying the hypothetical definition to the original descriptions
* identifying the structural definition

These activities were accomplished through a process that included intuiting, analyzing and describing in order to elicit the descriptive expressions and/or names of the elements. *Intuiting* is the process of understanding the phenomenon as described by the participant. Through the use of strict concentration and dedication to identification of the surfacing meaning of the phenomenon, the researcher was able to grasp the uniqueness of the phenomenon. *Describing* seeks to elicit the meaning of the elements of a lived experience. Descriptive statements can complete an idea about a lived experience. Common elements are abstract statements that are elicited from descriptive statements and result in major themes. These elements must be present either explicitly or implicitly in the majority of all descriptions. *Analyzing* explored the unique characteristics of the phenomenon and its association with other phenomena. Providing a description of the phenomena was accomplished when the researcher was able to sustain a connection between the phenomena and the terms used describe it.

From these themes and elements, a hypothetical definition of the phenomenon was derived. In steps five and six other experts were utilized to verify the descriptions made. These experts were experienced researchers familiar with the phenomenological process. The use of experts is imperative to test and retest the researcher's findings. This qualitative approach allowed the researcher an opportunity to study the emergence of themes and patterns of the lived experiences of an individual in a holistic manner.

Each of the audio tape recordings were transcribed, single spaced on half of the page vertically so as to allow the researcher space to write any additional thoughts and observations. Field notes were recorded for each interview which presented a more complete picture of each child. These field notes were incorporated into the analysis along with the verbal information obtained by the tape recordings.

Interviews were conducted with 9 children. Adequacy of the sample was achieved when redundancy or saturation was apparent. That is to say, that no new information was presented by any of the children and no new information related to the phenomenon was revealed.

Reliability and validity of qualitative research is enhanced by the researcher going back to the subjects with the hypothetical and structural definitions and validating with them whether in fact the researcher adequately described the meaning of the phenomena to the subject. Three of the nine subjects were still housed in the shelter when the hypothetical definitions were concluded and they agreed with the definition. The other six subjects had moved and left no forwarding address.

The principles of analysis as set forth by van Kaam were followed for this study. Strict adherence to those principles allowed the researcher to describe more fully the meaning and significance of homelessness for those children participating in this study.

Notes

1. B. Artinian, "Qualitative Modes of Inquiry," *Western Journal of Nursing Research* 10(2)(1988):138-149.

2. R. Parse, A. Coyne, and M. Smith, *Nursing Research: Qualitative Methods* (Bowie, MD:Prentice Hall, 1985).

3. L. Locke, W. Spirduso, and S. Silverman, *Proposals that Work*(2nd Ed.)(Newberry Park:SAGE Publications, 1987).

4. J. Lofland and L. Lofland, *Analyzing Social Settings: A Guide to Qualitative Observations and Analysis* (Belmont, CA:Wadsworth, 1984).

5. S. Faux, M. Walsh, and J. Deatrick, "Intensive Interviewing with Children and Adolescents, *Western Journal of Nursing Research* 10(2)(1988):180-184.

6. H.C. Becker, *Sociological Work* (Chicago:Aldine, 1970).

7. J. Rich, *Interviewing Children and Adolescents* (London:MacMillan, St. Martin Press, 1968).

8. L. Yarrow, "Interviewing Children," *Handbook of Research in Child Development*, P.H. Mussen, ed. (New York:John Wiley, 1960).

9. N. Babchuk and C.W. Gordon, "The Child as a Prototype of the Naive Informant in the Interview Situation," *American Sociological Review* 23(4)(1958):196-198.

10. G. Gorman, "The School-Age Child as Historian," *Pediatric Nursing* 5(1980):39-40.

11. E. Erikson, *Childhood and Society*(2nd Ed.)(New York:Norton Press, 1963).

12. P.H. Mussen, *Handbook of Research Methods in Child Development* (New York:Wiley, 1960).

13. B. Holiday and A. Turner-Henson, "Response Effects on a Survey with School-Age Children," *Nursing Research* 34(2)(1989):248-250.

14. J. Piaget, *The Construction of Reality in the Child*, M. Cook, translator (New York:Bevi Books, 1954).

15. A. van Kaam, *Existential Foundations of Psychology* (New York:Doubleday, 1969).

IV

The Findings

This chapter presents the data analysis and interpretation for the study entitled, "The meaning and significance of homelessness to a child." The philosophy, approach and methodological procedures of phenomenology suggested by van Kaam formed the guiding principles.[1] Included in this chapter are a profile of the participants and the analysis of the data including the descriptive expressions, common elements, themes, and a theoretical definition of the phenomenon.

Profile of the Participants

The study sample (Table 1) included nine children from two homeless shelters. Seven of the participants were African Americans and two were Caucasian. The children were all part of single parented family units headed by the biological mother. The children ranged in age from nine to 12 and represented five separate families. The children had been at the shelter for a period of time that ranged from four to nine weeks. The children's standing in school ranged from 1st to 5th grade. Five of the participants suggested that they had a chronic illness (asthma, 4; skin rashes, 3; and diabetes, 1). Of the homeless children that participated, six were female and three were males. Five of the children resided in the shelter in Jackson, Mississippi and four in the shelter in Marietta, Georgia. Only two of the mothers were working. One was a known drug abuser enrolled in an outpatient detoxification program and two of the mothers were currently receiving psychiatric outpatient care for conditions including depression and psychotic behavior. One child admitted to experimenting with alcohol, but none of the children were enrolled in a drug program or received psychiatric care.

The majority of the families (3 of the 5) were in the shelter due to situational homelessness, a traumatic episode of family violence. The other two families had been living with relatives, but due to a shortage of space or the longevity of that arrangement, had been asked to leave resulting in their residence in the shelter.

Analysis

Taped interviews with the nine children were transcribed and the significant statements extracted from these became the raw data for analysis. Significant or essential statements were those phrases and sentences that directly pertained to the meaning and impact of homelessness for these children.

Duplicate statements were eliminated if they contained some, or nearly all, of the same information of previous statements. These included 61 statements elicited from the transcriptions of the tape recordings with the children. Meanings were then formulated from the significant statements.   These meanings were derived following contemplative reading and rereading of the significant statements and reflecting back upon the original transcriptions so as to obtain the true meaning of the children's statements in the original context.

The formulated meanings were then organized into clusters of themes which emerged from, and were common to, all of the subjects descriptions. These clusters are presented in Table 2, A, B, and C. Once again, the researcher returned to the original transcriptions in order to validate the clusters. Each description was examined to ensure that the clusters of themes proposed thoughts that were in the original transcription and did not introduce ideas not contained in the original dialogue. An exhaustive definition of the phenomenon was achieved by the integration of the results of this analysis process.

A final validation was undertaken by returning to each of the shelters and attempting to locate the original subjects in order to discover if the definition formulated represented their actual experiences. Only three of the nine subjects could be located, but all of these agreed that the definition represented their experiences and the meaning and impact of homelessness for them. Additionally, this definition was presented to both shelter directors who were satisfied that the definition represented the essential meaning and impact of homelessness to the hundreds of children that they had seen over the years.

Interpretation

For the child who is homeless the meaning and impact of homelessness is derived from reciprocal knowing and understanding of the lived experience. This knowing and understanding was elicited from a synthesis of statements made by the children included in the sample as they related to the lived experience of homelessness.

Getting There

The first cluster, getting there, (Table 2A) described those events that occurred prior to becoming homeless as verbalized by each child. These events or life situations appeared to be elements associated with or precipitated by becoming homeless. These events comprised the first stage of homelessness for the children and they are thus described here as getting there.

Three themes were found in the cluster designated getting there. These were: how it happened, what it cost, and what was lost.

In the first theme, how it happened, the children described events that they perceived as precipitating coming to the shelter. Personal losses and violence were the most common subjects discussed by the children. Other subjects included frequent moves, living with relatives, getting evicted either by family or through circumstances and being afraid.

Situational homelessness is usually due to some event that causes individuals to suddenly and unexpectedly lose their residence or, in some cases, having to leave or flee their residence. For one child a violent act by her father precipitated coming to the shelter. This child described a particular act of physical violence against her mother by her father as being the reason for the family currently residing in the shelter. She stated:

> My dad shot my mom...then we had to leave. He used to hit her and all, all the time but then with the shooting we left our house and came here. He never hit us or anything but he always hit her and then the shooting. Well it was bad but we took his gun and then I got shot. See right here.(Pointing to her leg) I was really scared too but mamma said we would be safe here.

Living with relatives and friends is common in the homeless community. Friends and relatives frequently allow individuals to reside within their homes for an indefinite period of time but oftentimes resources begin to run out, overcrowding occurs or other situations force the individual, either through their own decision or that of the relative, to leave the home. One child described living with an uncle for a period of time stating:

> We used to live with my uncle. But....you know about what I said, he hurt me and then when mamma got mad he threw us out. (In a time out from the tape recorder the child reported to the researcher that she had been sexually abused by her uncle and his friends).We didn't have no place to go and he made us stay out in the street but then mamma said we was coming to Ms. Lida's house and then we would be OK.

She also added:

> We lived one time with grandma but then she went to California and now I don't know so we have to stay here. Daddy is in jail so we have to stay here.

Other children told similar stories of living with relatives or friends and finally, after a period of time, having to leave with no other residence but the shelter available to them. Another girl, aged 7, stated:

> One time we lived in a house, our house-then I don't know we lived with grandma. Then we had to go because nobody had any food so then we had to go. It's OK though cause we moves a lot.

For the majority of this sample of children, their resultant homeless state was due to an event or series of events that no longer allowed the family to independently maintain a residence. This is the case for most of the increasing number of homeless families.

Becoming homeless was sometimes a painful process for some of the children. Oftentimes individuals became homeless due to drug and alcohol related problems coupled with violence. In this sample, all of the children detailed some form of abuse, either that of drugs and alcohol or physical abuse. The children themselves sometimes became involved with drugs and ultimately suffered as a result of these behaviors. One boy aged 12 stated:

> We lived in a house with lots of people. There was lots of bad things there. Drinking and doping... all kinds of bad things. It was scary scary stuff...then all the fighting and then we had to go. Mamma had to be in the hospital and then when she got out we had nowhere to go so we came here. I tried some stuff too but it was bad.

Many factors were seen to play a part in the theme how it happened. In this sample, these included violence in the home, and physical, sexual, drug and alcohol abuse. The ultimate result was the loss of one's domicile.

The next theme that emerged from the data was what it cost. Homeless children typically exhibit below average school performance, poor health status and inadequate health maintenance practices, along with an increased incidence of chronic illness.

Most of the children talked about doing poorly in school or being held back a grade. One child stated:

> I stayed in the first grade two times but I'm gonna go to second grade this year. The teacher sent my mamma a good note this time and that's good.

Another child stated that he now attended school regularly. Irregular attendance is often the case for children who are homeless. He said:

> I used to not go cause everyone was stoned or something. Anyway, we were too tired sometimes. Now everyday we takes the bus and I goes to school now. I like it too.

And, finally, in another statement related to school a child aged nine said:

School is OK now but I didn't go too much before.
Now I'm learning how to write my name.

For those children exposed to drugs, alcohol, violence and life on the street, the loss of innocence was often evidenced in the manner in which a story was related to the researcher. Discussions about guns, shootings and the use of drugs were often stated in a matter of fact tone. Others seemed to perceive that their way of life was the norm.

Health was another area that had notable deficiencies for children who were homeless. Often, due to poor diet and environment, the lack of routine health care and the unavailability of medicines, the children exhibited poor health. When asked if they were often sick one child stated:

> I gets sick all the time. I have asthma too. Most of the time I don't have my medicine but now Ms. Lida gets it for me so I has it.

Another child who had eczema with secondary infection was asked about her health status. She stated:

> I has this rash all the time. I need some special medicine but I can't get it . Now the doctor at the clinic said some of these (pointing to sores on her body) are infected so I got a shot...but I had them a long time. Maybe now they will go away and stop hurting me too.

The most serious problem was discovered while interviewing a child who had diabetes. He said:

> I got the sugar but even if I have my medicine before we got no refrigerator so I couldn't use my medicine all the time. I got really sick one time and had to go to the hospital. But then my mamma said she'd do it (give the medicine) so I left the hospital. Now I'm OK but I hope when we move I have a refrigerator. Ms. Lida has one here so I keep my medicine in it and I'm not sick now.

For most of these children the needs mandated by chronic illness could not be met prior to coming to the shelter due to the inability to meet the most basic of needs: the lack of a home. Poor and inadequate diet, the lack of proper facilities for hygiene and medical care all contributed to these children's problems.

Most of the children could not remember going to the doctor regularly before coming to the shelter. There was little participation in any regular plan of health care, particularly health promotional activities. Getting there, or becoming homeless, was a treacherous journey filled with inadequacies in school, a diminished sense of self, increased violence, abuse, deficiencies in meeting the most basic of needs and, most importantly, a decreased sense of well-being.

The last theme in the first cluster was entitled what they lost. In this theme, the children's comments summarized all of the losses they had experienced in their lives.

Even in today's mobile society, most children enjoy some sense of family, friendships and normal age-related outlets. For these children, homelessness had caused the loss of family, friends and other age-appropriate social outlets. One child stated:

> I gots no friends really. Just a few kids here but
> most of them is babies and stuff. It's just me and my
> mamma now.

Only one of the children remembered ever having had a friend come over to play after school and none could remember going to another child's home after school. Other children spoke of the lack of toys and the rigid schedule that prevented them from enjoying things as simple as going to the movies. One child stated:

> There's a kid here-he has a Nintendo...but he doesn't
> let me play. Other than the Nintendo we got just a
> few baby toys and stuff but nothing for me. I watch
> the TV sometimes but its noisy in here (the central
> playroom) and I sure wanna play Nintendo. Anyway
> sometimes Ms. Lida will take us to the movies.

It was observed by the researcher that few of the toys were appropriate for children older than four or five years old. Additionally, the only television in the shelter was in the central dayroom where all the residents came to socialize.

Other costs included the loss of a sense of family. When asked about their families, few of the children could relate any recent contact with other family members or even current knowledge as to the whereabouts of any members of their extended family. One child, when asked about her family, thought for a very long time and finally said:

> My grandma is in California I think or somewhere.
> She is with one of the twins (her sister). But I don't
> know for sure. I don't know my daddy.

Only one of the children knew where his father was and related the following in answer to, "Do you know where your dad is now?"

> My daddy is in Parchman cause of the shooting. I
> can't see him anymore but I think my uncle or
> somebody lives here in Jackson.

In trying to follow up on the identity of the local relative the child stated:

> I don't know really who it is but I think somebody
> lives here but I never did see them.

The children's attitudes were again rather matter of fact regarding extended family members and none seemed overly concerned that they had no contact with any family members other than their mothers. For these children, there was a loss of both a supportive network of friends, family and an outlet for normal age related play.

Going Through It

The next cluster that emerged was going through it (Table 2B). This was seen as those realities associated with living each day at the shelter for the children. When asked to describe what their life was like now, the children described three distinct themes. These were: the best parts, the worst parts and, the everyday things.

The first theme in this cluster, the best parts, allowed the children an opportunity to comment on the positive aspects of their lives.

Many of the children described very positive feelings about their current life and all that it provided. All children commented on the amount and quality of the food now available for them. They also emphasized the fact that they were no longer scared and described a sense of semi permanence in their new "home". The fact that the children also all had a bed and some space for their family, along someone (Ms. Lida, the shelter director) who cared for them and their well being, was also evident in what was said. When one child was asked what the best parts of her life now were she excitedly replied:

> Oh! Oh! Oh, the food. There's a lot to eat here and there's a lot all the time.

When asked if this was different for them, having a lot of food, the same child stated:

> Oh yea...sometimes we had no food and you got really hungry.

Another child echoed these same thoughts stating:

> The best things here is that we gots lots of food and a bed. I like that.

This same child continued:

> Before to sleep I sleeps on the floor. We got no bed before here. Now I gots a room for me and mamma and the kids and a bed too. It's really nice. Do you want to see it?

Other comments were related to now having some space for their possessions and being safe. The instability of their former lives made existence at a shelter more acceptable for these children and offered them a sense of safety and security. It also provided a means to meet some of the more basic needs including housing, water, electricity, food and being part of a social system. The children in this sample seemed to be happier here than they had been in their previous residence and this was unanimously supported by all of the nine participants in the study.

While most of the children were satisfied with life at the shelter some did relate negative aspects of their life now. The second theme, the worst of it, echoed the thoughts and feelings related to the negative aspects of the children's lives. These negative aspects were seen as living in a crowded space with little opportunity for privacy, the lack and rarely, even the loss of a friend, the turnover of residents, which for some precipitated new losses, and the fear that soon they too would have to leave.

One child talked about a friend that he missed very much:

> Yea. I had a friend here but then it was time for him to go. We used to do things and stuff but now well you know, just lots a babies here. No more Pete. I really miss him a lot. Maybe when we go we could live with them or something. When we go I don't know where we's gonna live but Ms. Lida is going to help us I think. She helped Pete.

Other children suggested that the lack of privacy was a problem and shared that all in their family now lived in one room together. Other children talked about the one communal dayroom where it was hard to really think or hear the television because of the noise in the room.

These negative aspects of the children's lives, however, were not described with the same intensity as the positive aspects. The researcher noted that the children were often reluctant to discuss in detail any negative anecdotes and seemed to feel that these were minor inconveniences and that the best things more than made up for these few negative aspects.

The last theme in this cluster was entitled the everyday things. While people by nature are creatures of habit and routine, for these children the routine was often prescribed by the rules of the shelter. Oftentimes rigid schedules had to be adhered to in order to meet the needs of larger groups. The rules mandated that if the mother had a job her children had to go to a day care center until 5 PM when they would be picked up by either their mother or a shelter worker. Also, upon arrival at the shelter after school or daycare, all children must change into play clothes so as to spare their few suitable school clothes. All meals were served at a certain time and while some snacks were available in between meals, no means to obtain a meal that was missed were provided.

One child talked about having to go to daycare and stated:

> Yea, everyday I can't come home from I got to go with the babies. It's stupid. No snacks, eat at this time, change your clothes and go to the babysitter. I ain't no baby!

Going through it was a process that had positive and negative aspects for all the children. However, the positive aspects outweighed the negative and provided a means to satisfy some of the most basic needs such as food and shelter. While losses were experienced by some of the children and the lack of privacy and rigidity of schedules were seen as problems during this phase, going through it was, for all the children, a significant improvement over their lives prior to coming to the shelter.

GOING ON

The age old question of what do you want to be when you grow up is really a way for us to ask another, what do you see for the future? What are your hopes and dreams? For the children in this study the last cluster to emerge was going on (Table 2C), which provided the researcher with a way of examining how life seemed to the children now and in the future and revealed the children's hopes and dreams. How it is and hopes and dreams were the two themes that were contained in this cluster.

In order to come to an understanding of what the children's lives were like, the researcher attempted to see whether the children knew what the word homeless meant and then how it pertained to them. The first theme in this cluster, how it is, demonstrated the child's understanding of their life as it is now. Only one of the children could define the word homeless. Even when the researcher explained that homeless meant having no home, none of the children perceived themselves as homeless. One child, age 8, in answer to the question, "Where is your home now?" stated:

Silly, I live here. This is my home. Don't you
know that I live here!

The children were asked if they knew anyone who was homeless.
Of the nine children all but two replied no. The two both described an
elderly man who slept in a field near the shelter as being the only
person they knew who was homeless.

The one boy who was able to define homeless stated:

Well, being homeless means you got no home but the only
person I knows is the man in the field. Well maybe there's
the other mens at the Stewpot (a food pantry for homeless men
located across the street). But really I don't know none who
is homeless.

Another child said:

I don't know nobody cept maybe the men at the
Stewpot (a soup kitchen across the street) who are
homeless. We all gots a home right here.

In general, the children's comments supported the belief that they
were not homeless because they all had a home here at the shelter. In
these children's minds only people who lived out in the street were
perceived as homeless. While one of the children wished that they
could go back to their former house, they all shared the belief that this
was their home for now. It is noteworthy that none of the children
perceived themselves as homeless and all but two stated that they did
not know anyone who was homeless.

In the final theme, hopes and dreams, the children were asked
about their hopes and dreams and were given the hypothetical question,
"If you had one wish for the future, what would it be?" The answers
obtained were all similar in that their wishes centered around meeting
one's basic needs: economic stability, shelter, adequate nutrition and a
sense of well being. Some of the comments included:

(Boy, age 9) I wish we had lots of money. Then we
could gets all the things. You know a house and
food and we would be safe.

> (Girl, age 7) I wish I had a big car and a big house.
> Yeah, it would be a big blue house. But maybe just
> money cause then we could gets me and mamma a
> blue house, and a car and oh yeah, a pool too.

Other wishes were those which included having children their own age and sex with which to play. This is consistent with a child's need for peer group interaction. One 11 year old boy stated:

> I wish there were more boys for me to play with.
> You know since Pete moved from here I gots no one
> at all now so I wish for money and a friend.

Wishes for the future, therefore, for these homeless children included those things that could satisfy an individual's basic material and personal needs.

Based on the findings from this study, homelessness was viewed as a three staged process which began with those events that preceded becoming homeless, followed by that period of time that they were at the shelter and finally concluded with the children's dreams for the future. Although the events in their lives were often described in flat and unemotional tones by the children, their lives had indeed been changed dramatically by the phenomenon of homelessness. While the unemotional tones suggested that the children may have viewed their lives as normal, their wishes and dreams all described deficits in their lives that were seeking a home, safety, and security.

Description of the Phenomenon

As a result of an integration of the findings of the analysis a hypothetical and structural definition of the phenomenon were constructed. These definitions of the meaning and impact of homelessness for a child were as follows.

Hypothetical definition

For a child, homelessness was viewed as a disruptive event in a normal life pattern which caused deficits in one's most basic needs: security, health, nutrition and peer and family relationships. Violence and isolation often caused or preceded homelessness. Homelessness was a phenomenon accompanied by, and often the cause of, the breakdown of families, an increased incidence of chronic illness, poor school performance and the lack of a significant peer group.

Homelessness altered a child's wishes and dreams, which for the homeless child included fewer self-centered wishes. Instead, more emphasis was placed on those that would satisfy one's basic needs and increase stability in their lives.

Structural definition

The results of this research are summarized by the structural definition. In this study homelessness, therefore, was not perceived as a lack of a home but a lack of structure, filled with deficits and disruptions that diminished a child's life.

Notes

1. A. van Kaam, *Existential Foundations of Psychology* (New York:Doubleday, 1969).

V

Conclusions, Implications,
and Recommendations

The purpose of this study was to define the meaning and significance of homelessness to a child. Nine children who were homeless were interviewed utilizing a phenomenological approach. The synthesis of this analysis revealed that homelessness was a multistage process that began with those events that preceded and, for many of the children, caused their homelessness. This multistage process continued during the period of time that they were homeless and was further evidenced by the impact that the phenomenon had on their physical, emotional and developmental well-being as well as their hopes and dreams for the future. Homelessness was associated with violence, isolation, the breakdown of families, an increased incidence of chronic illness, poor school performance and a lack of a significant peer group. For homeless children, homelessness was not perceived as a lack of a home, but rather a lack of structure, filled with deficits and disruptions that diminished the quality of a child's life.

This chapter will provide conclusions based on the findings of this study and show how these relate to the current literature. In addition, it will present the implications of these findings for nursing and provide recommendations for future study.

Conclusions

While homelessness is defined as being without a permanent domicile that can be secured without special assistance, the children in this study did not perceive themselves as being homeless.[1] Instead, the children viewed the shelter as their permanent domicile (*i.e.* their tangible and intangible for the children. Analysis of the data revealed three clusters and nine themes that defined the meaning and significance of homelessness for a child. The phenomenon was seen as a multistage process that began with those events included in the first cluster *(getting there)*, followed by those perceptions of their lives at the present time the second cluster *(being there)* and concluded with those hopes and dreams for the future as verbalized by the children in the last cluster *(going on)*.

The sample was characteristic of the current demographic profile of homeless families cited in the literature: single parented families with the mother being the head of a household with approximately 2.5 children.[2] Nearly all the children had prior recollections of living with other relatives and a few remembered a residence that was not shared with other families prior to coming to the shelter. All of the children described multiple prior moves.[3]

For the children in this study, violence, abuse (both physical and sexual) and the breakdown of families were the most significant parts of the first stage of homelessness, getting there. This finding is validated by previous research which states that homelessness may sometimes be a gradual process evidenced by the breakdown of families, domestic violence, unexpected family or economic crisis, drug and alcohol abuses as well as other forms of violence and abuse.[4] Homelessness often results in living in a chaotic and inconsistent environment with families frequently seeking shelters as a temporary solution to their problems.[5] This was the case for all nine children interviewed in this study. These families had all experienced some form of violence or other crisis that left them with only one alternative if they were not to live in the street, a shelter for the homeless.

The data suggested that, particularly in the case of households headed by single mothers, additional assistance in life, parenting, job preparation, and survival skills are needed. This assistance could be provided by school programs or job training programs at the shelters themselves. It is essential for health care providers to understand the multiple stressors faced by the children themselves and the special needs that they have. This understanding can increase the health care provider's ability to provide both appropriate and often timely care. The lack of adequate support systems was particularly obvious in this sample of homeless children. Not only was there a dysfunctional family unit, but there was a lack of peers with whom the children could play and interact as well as seek emotional support, hampering their ability to achieve their age appropriate developmental tasks. Bassuk & Rubin,[6] Rescoria et al.,[7] and Bassuk & Rosenberg,[8] Terrell[9] reported that homeless children had a significantly higher number of developmental delays than children who were housed. The present study supports previous ones which have concluded that although many of the children were "street wise", few had accomplished those tasks considered appropriate for the latency stage of middle childhood (industry versus inferiority) as described by Erikson.[10]

The children in this study had a low sense of self-worth, no significant peer group interactions, delays in personal, health and school achievements, as well as a negative social environment that was not conducive to their achieving a sense of accomplishment. Often, these children had inappropriate concerns for their age such as where would they live next, how could they seek an adequate source of food and would they be safe. The lack of privacy, structure and often, the acutely stressful experiences that had brought them to the shelter, all negatively impacted their ability to accomplish normal developmental tasks. The situations in which they lived prior to coming to the shelter as well as the chaotic nature of the shelter then became the model for their development. Bandura stressed that children model the adults and environment in which they live.[11] If this is accepted as true, then the health care provider must begin to seek ways to intervene and normalize the environment for children by providing more appropriate models for them.

In the next stage which emerged as the cluster, going through it, the children related both positive and negative attributes of being sheltered and homeless. While the literature suggests that, even in a shelter, nutritional needs of children are often poorly met,[12] for these children, having regular meals was seen in a positive light and the nutritional content was viewed as unimportant. However, meeting nutritional requirements of children is a critical need and has a great effect on both their physical and mental abilities.[13]

The literature indicates that the multiple prior moves and crowded, chaotic living quarters where several families live together are commonly part of the experience among homeless children. Although their new shelter home provided a small space which usually lacked privacy, the experience of having a space to share with only their immediate family members was seen as a positive attribute of their new environment.

Lack of peer companionship, the loss of a stable and complete family and the limited activities appropriate for school-aged children were all viewed as negative aspects of the children's lives. Many had only vague memories of family members and fewer had any current knowledge about their extended families. The lack of a peer group from which the children could seek companionship and validation of their accomplishments was apparent in all of the children interviewed. Furthermore, the lack of appropriate recreational outlets provided even fewer opportunities for these children. With the literature consistently citing developmental delays as common for homeless children, the experiences of these children are in agreement and perhaps provide evidence as to why developmental delays are so common among homeless children. Within a negative or limited environment and social setting of the shelter, these children do not have ample opportunity to grow and accomplish the developmental tasks expected of their age group. The development of a sense of industry comes from accomplishments within one's own experience. For the children in this sample who had no extended family, few friends, a notable lack of a significant support system, less than optimal recreational opportunities, and poor health and school performance, the development of a sense of accomplishment or the achievement of industry was unlikely. Rather, a sense of inferiority was felt to exist in these children who had so many negative factors in their lives.

Going through it, the second stage of homelessness for these children, was seen by the children as both a negative and positive phase. This stage presented many opportunities for health care providers working with these children and suggested that interventions which may improve outcomes for homeless children should be implemented. These could include improving the environment so that emotional, physical and developmental needs are better met and performing a more complete evaluation of children that come to the shelter so that appropriate strategies can be put in place to optimize their potential for growth and development.

Finally, in the last stage of homelessness *(going on)* that emerged from the data, the children's hopes for the future were echoed in their wishes and dreams. This last stage provided the researcher with a unique opportunity to hear the children's hopes expressed in totally unselfish terms that were directed at stabilizing their own families. Their wishes, which included food, shelter or a home of their own, economic stability, safety and quiet seemed to summarize all that was missing in their lives now. This lack of selfish demands or wishes was also found by Rescoria et al.

The findings of this phenomenological study added to the limited research related to homeless children. The study provided a unique insight into what it means for a child to be homeless and how these children were impacted by this phenomenon. The results supported the premise that homelessness is a state of being which is often precipitated by actions over which children have no power. Domestic violence, drug abuse, joblessness and the lack of affordable, available housing were identified by the child as the precursors for homelessness. The results of being homeless were often evidenced by the child's lack of family structure, few friends, poor health and school performance and the loss of childhood dreams. Interventions at both the first and second stage of homelessness are needed in order to break the cycle of homelessness. These findings have implications for the areas of nursing education, practice, research and in the building and testing of theory.

Nursing Education

The findings of this study should be included in both undergraduate and graduate education. While a general understanding of both children's developmental and health needs is provided in most nursing programs, nursing students should become more cognizant of the special needs of homeless children. Since homeless children and their families are the fastest growing segment of a population whose numbers are expected to exceed 1 million within the next decade, it is important for educators to recognize this as a special population with unique needs.[14] The lack of family and friends decreases a child's sense of trust and belonging, making it difficult for the child to accept the nurse in any health care setting. Delayed developmental status and increased health needs are common among homeless children therefore mandating a special or different approach when dealing with these children.[15]

Much like the cycle of battering, homelessness for many of these children is the norm and is likely to be repeated in the next generation; therefore, educators must become more aware of interventions that help break the cycle. Nurse educators need to continue to be cognizant of social problems that impact the client and ultimately alter the way that nurses and nursing students interact with those clients.

Nursing Research

The findings from this study support those of Faux et al.,[16] Yarrow,[17] Becker,[18] Lofland & Lofland,[19] and Artinian[21] by demonstrating that valid data can be gathered directly from children. While this study provided insights as to what it means to be a homeless child, clearly, further research is needed to understand the stages of homelessness as perceived by these children.

The suggestion that homelessness may be a phenomenon that is cyclic in nature also needs further investigation either by means of a longitudinal or retrospective study. Quantitative research should be the next step based on the results of this qualitative study, and should be specifically related to health and developmental needs, social policy, family structure and values. A quantitative testing of the model of homelessness proposed here using other homeless children could provide badly needed information for nursing science, leading to a clearer understanding of meaningful interventions for the homeless child.

Nursing Practice

The fact that each client is unique and has his or her own perceptions and reality are essential concepts to understand in nursing practice. While it is logical to assume that each individual is the best source of information about that individual's experiences, oftentimes children are not approached in the same manner as adults. Caregivers are usually asked to provide information about children; however, this study allowed the insight that the child himself can provide a unique insight that the caregiver may not be aware of or understand.

Nurses in practice need to be more aware of the increased risks and incidence for disease, both chronic and acute, in populations of homeless children. Furthermore, the nurse must remain cognizant of the fact that the decreased support systems and lack of environmental support may impact treatment regimes and compliance among this population.

Many practice opportunities are suggested by this study. The results validate the need for increased health supervision at day care centers, schools and homeless shelters. For the homeless child who is dependent on adult caregivers, providing care must occur at the shelters rather than relying on an already stressed caregiver to get the children to yet another clinic site where help may be obtained.[210] Nursing clinics managed by nurse practitioners in schools, daycare centers and shelters may provide an ideal solution for many of these underserved children.

Nursing Theory

Rogers[22] and Bandura served as the theoretical frameworks for this study. Rogers states that man and his environment are continuously exchanging matter and energy and when a person is in synchrony with the environment a state of optimal health can be obtained. Conversely, she maintains that when deficits in one's environment exist it is impossible to reach one's maximal potential for health and well being. For the homeless children in this study environmental disequilibrium was evidenced in nearly every aspect of their life. These included health, school performance, emotional state, developmental stage, and family ties. Therefore, within this framework, nurses' attitudes and behaviors need to include those which can assist the child in creating a pattern of synchrony and organization for the client so as to assist these children in reaching their maximum health potential.

When one examines the impact of Bandura's theory of development, it is clear that modeling of behaviors occurs in all children and is the way in which knowledge, behaviors and attitudes are learned.[12] For the children included in this study, the sense of normalcy when discussing violence and abusive situations and the flat and emotionally devoid descriptions of losses and the sense of futility echoed in their words, should send a warning to those who care for them. Not only have these children been negatively impacted by their environment, but the models from which all their formative learning is to be accomplished lack the appropriate activities from which they can learn socially acceptable behaviors. The environment in which these children grow up lacks the models that allow them to learn the skills needed to accomplish the tasks of industry because the adults in their world have no sense of accomplishment themselves.

This study clearly validates both Roger's and Bandura's frameworks by providing a picture of a group of children who, subjected to a deficient environment devoid of appropriate role models, have numerous deficits themselves and nearly all of whom have failed to accomplish the task of industry or accomplishment. The nurse's actions and attitudes can not only become a new role model for the children, but can also become a medium through which synchrony can be achieved and outcomes for these children can be significantly improved.

Recommendations

The following recommendations for further study are suggested by this research:

* A replication of this study with a larger sample.
* An investigation into the hypothesis that homelessness is cyclic in nature by means of either a longitudinal or retrospective study.
* An intervention study which tests the hypothesis that developmental lags and physical problems can be modified if assistance is given on site where the children are housed; the experimental design should compare outcomes of children who have been given adequate opportunities against those who have not.
* Conduction of a study that attempts to quantify the phenomenon of homelessness by collecting data appropriate for formulating indices for evaluation.

Notes

1. United States Congress, House of Delegates, Select Committee on Hunger, *Hunger among the Homeless: A Survey of 140 Shelters, Food Stamp Participation and Recommendations* (Washington, D.C.:United States Government, 1984):7-40.

2. J. Murata, J. Mace, A. Stretlow, and P. Schuler, *Journal of Pediatric Nursing* 7(3)(1992):196-203.

3. C. Adkins and J. Fields, "Health Care Values of Homeless Women and their Children," *Family and Community Health* (1992).

4. E. Bassuk and L. Rosenberg, "Psychosocial Characteristics of Homeless Children and Children with Homes," *Pediatrics* 85(3)(1990):257-261.

5. E. Bassuk and L. Rosenberg, "Why Does Family Homelessness Occur? A Case-Control Study," *American Journal of Public Health* 78(7)(1988):783-788.

6. S. Damrosche, P. Sullivan, A. Scholler, and J. Gaines, "On Behalf of Homeless Families," *Journal of Maternal Child Nursing* 13(5)(1988):256-263.

7. L. Rescoria, R. Parker, and P. Stolley, "Ability, Achievement and Adjustment in Homeless Children," *American Journal of Orthopsychiatry* 6(2)(1991):210-220.

8. E. Bassuk and L. Rubin, "Homeless Children: A Neglected Population," *American Journal of Orthopsychiatry* 57(2)(1987): 279-286.

9. C. Terrell, *Developmental Levels of Children who are Classified as Homeless and Children who are not Classified as Homeless* (Unpublished master's thesis, Mississippi University for Women, Columbus, MS, 1993).

10. E. Erikson, *Childhood and Society*(2nd Ed.) (New York:Norton Press, 1963).

11. A. Bandura, *Social Learning Theory* (Englewood Cliffs, N.J.:Prentice Hall, 1977).

12. J. Bass, P. Brennan, K. Mehta, and S. Kodzis, "Pediatric Problems in a Suburban Shelter for Homeless Families," *Pediatrics* 85(10)(1990):33-39.

13. A. Casey, "An Oasis in the Streets," *California Nurses Review* 11(1)(1989):46.

14. D.R. Hodnicki, "Homelessness: Health Care Implications," *Journal of Community Health Care* 7(2)(1990):59-67.

15. J. Wright and E. Weber, *Homelessness and Health* (New York:McGraw Hill, 1988).

16. S. Faux, M. Walsh, and J. Deatrick, "Intensive Interviewing with Children and Adolescents," *Western Journal of Nursing Research* 10(2)(1988):180-184.

17. L. Yarrow, "Interviewing Children," *Handbook of Research in Child Development*, P.H. Mussen, ed. (New York:John Wiley, 1960).

18. H.C. Becker, *Sociological Work* (Chicago:Aldine, 1970).

19. J. Lofland and L. Lofland, *Analyzing Social Settings: A Guide to Qualitative Observations and Analysis* (Belmont, CA: Wadsworth, 1984).

20. B. Artinan, "Qualitative Modes of Inquiry," *Western Journal of Nursing Research* 10(2)(1988):138-149.

21. L.J. Pearson, "Providing Health Care to the Homeless-Another Important Role for NPs," *Nurse Practitioner* 13(4)(1988): 38-48.

22. M. Rogers, *An Introduction to the Theoretical Basis of Nursing* (Philadelphia:F.A. Davis, 1970).

Appendix A

Interview Guide

The following questions have been prepared to serve as an interview guide for the investigation into the meaning and significance of homelessness to children. It is meant to assist the researcher in eliciting the expressed cognitive, personal, affective, and physical responses of the child to their current situation of being without a permanent domicile. When using this tool, some of the language may have to be modified to suit the developmental level of the individual child. The researcher may use all or part of the questions that follows and this should be determined by each individual interview.

The guide asks questions related to personal responses, the effect homelessness has had on religious health, emotional, familial, community, and personal responses of the child. The guide also provides an opportunity to discuss past patterns and future hopes of the child. Careful attention should be made to the physical responses that may be observed by the research and those should be noted.

1. How long have you been at this shelter?

2. Where were you before you came to this shelter? Can you tell me about that place?

3. Tell me what you like most about being at this shelter. Can you tell me more about those things?

4. Tell me what you do not like about this shelter. Can you tell me more about those things?

5. Tell me how your life has changed or what is different for you since you came to this shelter.

6. Can you tell me about your friends? (Who are they? What kinds of things do you do together?)

7. Tell me about your family. Can you tell me where they are now? Do you want to share some stories with me about them?

8. Do you go to school now? (If not, where did you go before you came here?) Can you tell me what is like at school?

9. Do you go to any particular church? Can you tell me more about your church?

10. Can you tell me about your health? Have you been sick lately? Do you take any medicine? Have you been in the hospital?

11. Now, can you tell me anything else about yourself...Maybe, like what do you like to do, or where do you like to go, play, or be? What is your favorite television show?

12. Let us say that you just got up in the morning. Can you tell me what is your whole day?

13. Can you tell me what is means to be homeless? Do you know anyone who is homeless? Where is your home?

14. And finally, if you could have one wish in the whole world, what would it be?

Appendix B

Child's Assent Form

Child's Assent Form

I _____, state that I am ____ years of age and would like to take part in the program of research by Linda Sullivan, R.N.

The purpose of the research is to learn more about what it is like to be a child in a homeless shelter.

This study involves about one hour of my time. I will answer some questions and talk with Mrs. Sullivan, a registered nurse, and everything we say will be tape recorded.

No one but Mrs. Sullivan will know what is said.

If I have any questions, I can ask my parent(s) or Mrs. Sullivan.

No one is making me do this and I can stop any time I want to.

The answers that I give will be used to help people that take care of children learn more about what it is like living in a homeless shelter.

Date: _____   Subject Signature:_____
                           Researcher Signature:_____

Adapted from Faux, Walsh, Deatrick, 1988.

Appendix C

Parental Consent Form

Parental Consent Form

I am a registered nurse and a graduate student at the University of Alabama at Birmingham. As part of my doctoral studies, I am conducting a research project on the meaning and significance of homelessness to children. The results of this study will provide a better understanding of the health, emotional, developmental, and social needs of children who are living in a homeless shelter for health care providers.

I would like you permission to tape an interview with your child during which they will express the significance and meaning of homelessness to a child. All the information obtained during this interview will be kept strictly confidential and both your's and your child's identity will not be disclosed.

Your child's participation is strictly voluntary and will not affect your status at this shelter. You may choose to withdraw your child from this study at any time. After analysis of the data is completed, your child's tape will be destroyed. A summary of the results can be made available to you upon completion of the study if you desire.

Please feel free to contact me for further information at (601) 323-9365. Thank you for considering this request.

Sincerely,

Linda Sullivan, R.N., C., M.S.N.

I have read all the above, asked questions, received answers concerning areas that I did not understand, and am willing to give consent for my child to participate in this study.

Signature	Date

Researcher	Date

Appendix D

Institutional Review
Board Approval Form

**THE UNIVERSITY OF
ALABAMA AT BIRMINGHAM**

Office of the Institutional Review Board for Human Use

FORM 4: IDENTIFICATION AND CERTIFICATION OF
RESEARCH PROJECTS INVOLVING HUMAN SUBJECTS

THE INSTITUTIONAL REVIEW BOARD (IRB) MUST COMPLETE THIS FORM FOR ALL APPLI-
CATIONS FOR RESEARCH AND TRAINING GRANTS, PROGRAM PROJECT AND CENTER GRANTS,
DEMONSTRATION GRANTS, FELLOWSHIPS, TRAINEESHIPS, AWARDS, AND OTHER PROPOSALS
WHICH MIGHT INVOLVE THE USE OF HUMAN RESEARCH SUBJECTS INDEPENDENT OF SOURCE
OF FUNDING.

THIS FORM DOES NOT APPLY TO APPLICATIONS FOR GRANTS LIMITED TO THE SUPPORT
OF CONSTRUCTION, ALTERATIONS AND RENOVATIONS, OR RESEARCH RESOURCES.

PRINCIPAL INVESTIGATOR: LINDA SULLIVAN

PROJECT TITLE: THE MEANING AND SIGNIFICANCE OF HOMELESSNESS TO A CHILD

_____1.   THIS IS A TRAINING GRANT. EACH RESEARCH PROJECT INVOLVING HUMAN
          SUBJECTS PROPOSED BY TRAINEES MUST BE REVIEWED SEPARATELY BY THE
          INSTITUTIONAL REVIEW BOARD (IRB).

__X__2.   THIS APPLICATION INCLUDES RESEARCH INVOLVING HUMAN SUBJECTS. THE
          IRB HAS REVIEWED AND APPROVED THIS APPLICATION ON JULY 08, 1992
          IN ACCORDANCE WITH UAB'S ASSURANCE APPROVED BY THE UNITED STATES
          PUBLIC HEALTH SERVICE. THE PROJECT WILL BE SUBJECT TO ANNUAL
          CONTINUING REVIEW AS PROVIDED IN THAT ASSURANCE.

          _____   THIS PROJECT RECEIVED EXPEDITED REVIEW.

          __X__   THIS PROJECT RECEIVED FULL BOARD REVIEW.

_____3.   THIS APPLICATION MAY INCLUDE RESEARCH INVOLVING HUMAN SUBJECTS.
          REVIEW IS PENDING BY THE IRB AS PROVIDED BY UAB'S ASSURANCE.
          COMPLETION OF REVIEW WILL BE CERTIFIED BY ISSUANCE OF ANOTHER
          FORM 4 AS SOON AS POSSIBLE.

_____4.   EXEMPTION IS APPROVED BASED ON EXEMPTION CATEGORY NUMBER(S)_____.

DATE: JULY 08, 1992

Russell Cunningham M.D.
RUSSELL CUNNINGHAM/ M.D.
INTERIM CHAIRMAN OF THE
INSTITUTIONAL REVIEW BOARD

The University of Alabama at Birmingham
212 Mortimer Jordan Hall • 1825 University Boulevard • UAB Station
Birmingham, Alabama 35294-2010 • (205) 934-3789 • FAX (205) 934-7841

Appendix E

Mississippi Shelter
Approval Form

Agency Consent Form

Title of the Study: An inquiry into the meaning and significance of homelessness to children: a qualitative approach.

My name is Linda Sullivan. I am a registered nurse, certified family nurse practitioner and a doctoral candidate at the University of Alabama. I am currently investigating the impact of the homeless experience on children. The results of this study will be used by health care providers to better understand the effect of the homeless experience on children and it is hoped to therefore provide better care for these children. A copy of the results of this study will be available at your request.

I would like your written permission that you will support this study by allowing me access to children currently residing in your shelter. Each child will be interviewed and their conversations will be tape recorded. These recordings will then be analyzed by the researcher. The anonymity of the child will be protected at all times. Children will be asked to sign or otherwise acknowledge by use of an assent form and at least one parent will be asked to sign a consent form.

Your assistance with this study is greatly appreciated. Please sign below as indicated and return this form in its entirety to be in the enclosed envelop. Thank you for your participation.

I, _Lida Caraway_, acting in the capacity of _Director_ hereby give my permission for the children in this shelter to participate in this research study.

Date: _09/09/92_

Date: _Sept 9, 1992_

Signature: _Lida Caraway_
Name of facility _Sims House_
Address _1010 West Capitol / Jackson_ 39203
Phone _969-3487_
Researcher: _Linda Sullivan_

Appendix F

Georgia Shelter
Approval Form

Title of the Study: An inquiry into the meaning and significance of homelessness to children: a qualitative approach.

My name is Linda Sullivan. I am a registered nurse, certified family nurse practitioner and a doctoral candidate at the University of Alabama. I am currently investigating the impact of the homeless experience on children. The results of this study will be used by health care providers to better understand the effect of the homeless experience on children and it is hoped to therefore provide better care for these children. A copy of the results of this study will be available at your request.

I would like your written permission that you will support this study by allowing me access to children currently residing in your shelter. Each child will be interviewed and their conversations will be tape recorded. These recordings will then be analyzed by the researcher. The anonymity of the child will be protected at all times. Children will be asked to sign or otherwise acknowledge by use of an assent form and at least one parent will be asked to sign a consent form.

Your assistance with this study is greatly appreciated. Please sign below as indicated and return this form in its entirety to be in the enclosed envelop. Thank you for your participation.

I _Nancy Merrie_, acting in the capacity of _Executive Director of M.U.S.T._ hereby give my permission for the children in this shelter to participate in this research study.

Date: _April 20, 1992_

Date: _April 27, 1992_

Signature: _Nancy Merrie_
Name of facility _Clipboard Inn_
Address _55 Clarbot Church St Marietta Ga 30060_
Phone _(404) 627-1282_
Researcher: _Linda Sullivan_

Ministries United For Service and Training

P.O. Box 1717
Marietta, Georgia 30061
427-9862

Ms. Linda Sullivan R.N.,C.,M.S.N.   April 20, 1992
Mississippi University for Women
Columbus, MS 39701

Dear Ms. Sullivan,

    Enclosed please find the agency request form you submitted to
us. Permission has been granted to me to proceed per our telephone
conversation and your follow up letter dated April 9, 1992.
    I look forward to working with you over the coming months.

                                        Sincerely,

                                        Tom Plamann
                                        Director
                                        Daybreak Center at M.U.S.T.

Table 1

Profile of Participants

Race: 7 African American
                   2 Caucasian

Age: 9 to 12 years

Illness Profile   Chronic illness
in 5 of the 9:   Asthma
                   Diabetes
                   Eczema
                   Dermatitis
                   Psoriasis

Time in Shelter: 4 to 9 weeks

Grade   First and Fifth Grade
in School:

Gender: 6 Females
                   3 Males

* All were children of single parent (mother only) families.

Table 2A

Cluster Number 1

Cluster	Theme	Significant Statement
	How It Happened	Personal Violation
		Being Afraid
		Multiple Moves
		Abuse/Violence
		Getting Thrown Out
		Getting Too Crowded
Getting There	What it Cost	Poor School Performance
		Increased Illness
		Poor Health Maintenance
		Support Group
		Spiritual/Family Life
	What They Lost	Family Connections
		Friends
		Play Opportunities
		A Sense of Innocence

Table 2B

Cluster Number 2

Cluster	Theme	Significant Statement
		Safety
		A Bed of My Own
		Stability
	The Best	Someone Who Cares
	Parts	Having More Food
		Having a Home
		Making Friends
		Lack of Privacy
		Too Few Friends
Being There	The Worst	Moving Again
	Parts	Too Many Babies
		More Losses
		Crowded/Small Space
		A Loss of "Sense of Time"
		Changing Clothes
	Everyday	Going to Day Care
		Eating Regimens
		Rigid Schedule
		The Sameness

Table 2C

Cluster Number 3

Cluster	Theme	Significant Statement
		Now Having a Home
		Only People Who Live in the Street are Homeless
	How It Is	Wishing for Their Former Homes
		Moving Again
Going On		
		Selfless Wishes
		Security
		Big Blue House
	Hopes and Dreams	Stability
		Friends/Playmates
		Money
		Cars

References

Adkins, C. and J.Field, "Health Care Values of Homeless Women and Their Children," *Family and Community Health* (1992).

Artinian, B., "Qualitative Modes of Inquiry," *Western Journal of Nursing Research* 10(2)(1988):138-149.

Bandura, A., *Social Learning Theory* (Englewood Cliffs, N.J.:Prentice Hall, 1977).

Babchuk, N. and C.W. Gordon, "The Child as a Prototype of the Naive Informant in the Interview Situation," *American Sociological Review* 23(4)(1958):196-198.

Bassuk, E., "The Homeless Population," *Scientific American* 251(1)(1984):40-45.

Bass, J., Brenna, P., K. Mehata, and S. Kodzi, "Pediatric Problems in a Suburban Shelter for Homeless Families," *Pediatrics* 85(1)(1990):33-39.

Bassuk, E. and L. Rosenberg, "Why Does Family Homelessness Occur? A Case-Control Study," *American Journal of Public Health* 78(7)(1988):783-788.

Bassuk, E., and L. Rosenberg, "Psychosocial Characteristics of Homeless Children and Children with Homes," *Pediatrics* 85(3)(1990):257-261.

Bassuk, E., and L. Rubin, "Homeless Children: A Neglected Population," *American Journal of Orthopsychiatry* 57(2)(1987): 279-286.

Becker, H.C., *Sociological Work* (Chicago:Aldine, 1970). J. Murata, J. Mace, A. Stretlow, and P. Schuler, *Journal of Pediatric Nursing* 7(3)(1992):196-203.

Breakey, W., and P. Fischer, "Down and Out in a Land of Plenty," *Johns Hopkins Magazine* 37(1985):16-24.Casey, "An Oasis in the Streets," *California Nurses Review* 11(1)(1989):p.46.

Erikson, E., *Childhood and Society*(2nd Ed.) (New York:Norton Press, 1963).

Faux, S., Walsh, M., and J. Deatrick, "Intensive Interviewing with Children and Adolescents," *Western Journal of Nursing Research* 10(2)(1988):180-184.

Gorman, G., "The School-Age Child as Historian," *Pediatric Nursing* 5(1980):39-40.

Haase, J. and S. Myers, "Reconciling Paradigm Assumptions of Qualitative Research, *Western Journal of Nursing Research* 10(2)(1988):128-137.

Hodnicki, D.R., "Homelessness: Health Care Implications," *Journal of Community Health Care* 7(2)(1990):59-67.

Holiday, A., and A. Turner-Henson, "Response Effects on a Survey with School-Age Children," *Nursing Research*

Kinzel, D., "Self identified Health Concerns of Two Homeless Groups," *Western Journal of Nursing Research* 13(2)(1991):181-184.

Locke,L., W. Spirduso, and S. Silverman, *Proposals that Work*(2nd Ed.)(Newberry Park:SAGE Publications, 1987).

Lofland, J., and L. Lofland, *Analyzing Social Settings: A Guide to Qualitative Observations and Analysis* (Belmont, CA: Wadsworth, 1984).

Piaget, J., *The Construction of Reality in the Child*, M. Cook, translator (New York:Bevi Books, 1954).

Marriner, A., *Nursing Theorists and Their Work* (St. Louis: C. V. Mosby, 1986).

Mussen, P.H., *Handbook of Research Methods in Child Development* (New York:Wiley, 1960).

Parker, R., L. Rescoria, J. Finklestein, and N. Barnes, "A Survey of Health of Homeless Children in Philadelphia Shelters," *American Journal of Diseases in Children* 14(1991):20-526.

Parse,R., A. Coyne, and M. Smith, *Nursing Research: Qualitative Methods* (Bowie, MD:Prentice Hall, 1985).

Damrosche, S., P. Sullivan, A. Scholler, and J. Gaines, "On Behalf of Homeless Families," *Journal of Maternal Child Nursing* 13(5)(1988):256-263.

Pearson, L.J., "Providing Health Care to the Homeless-Another Important Role for NP's," *Nurse Practitioner* 13(4)(1988):38-48.

Rescoria, L., R. Parker, and P. Stolley, "Ability, Achievement and Adjustment in Homeless Children," *American Journal of Orthopsychiatry* 6(2)(1991):210-220.

Rich, J., *Interviewing Children and Adolescents* (London:MacMillan, St. Martin Press, 1968).

Rogers, M., *An Introduction to the Theoretical Basis of Nursing* (Philadelphia:F. A. Davis, 1970).

Rogers, M., *Visions of Science Based Nursing* (New York: National League for Nursing, 1990).

Terrell, C., *Developmental Levels of Children who are Classified as Homeless and Children who are not Classified as Homeless* (Unpublished master's thesis, Mississippi University for Women, Columbus, MS, 1993).

United States Congress, House of Delegates, Select Committee on Hunger, *Hunger among the Homeless: A Survey of 140 Shelters, Food Stamp Participation and Recommendations* (Washington, D.C.:United States Government, 1987), 7-40.

van Kaam, A., *Existential Foundations of Psychology* (New York:Doubleday, 1969).

Wright, J. and E. Weber, *Homelessness and Health* (New York:McGraw Hill, 1988).

Yarrow, L., "Interviewing Children," *Handbook of Research in Child Development*, P.H. Mussen, ed. (New York:John Wiley, 1960).

Index